The
Secretary's
Secret
Weapon

The
Secretary's
Secret
Weapon

Arm Yourself for Success
With Seven Essential
Communication Skills

BOBBI LINKEMER

amacom
American Management Association

New York • Atlanta • Boston • Chicago • Kansas City • San Francisco • Washington, D.C.
Brussels • Mexico City • Tokyo • Toronto

This publication is designed to provide accurate and authoritative information in regard to the subject matter covered. It is sold with the
understanding that the publisher is not engaged in rendering legal,
accounting, or other professional service. If legal advice or other expert
assistance is required, the services of a competent professional person
should be sought.

Library of Congress Cataloging-in-Publication Data

Linkemer, Bobbi.
    The secretary's secret weapon : arm yourself for success with
seven essential communication skills / Bobbi Linkemer.
        p.   cm.
    Includes bibliographical references and index.
    ISBN 0-8144-7895-6 (pbk.)
    1. Secretaries.   2. Business communication.   3. Interpersonal
communication.   I. Title.
    HF5547.5.L564   1996
    650.14'08'8651—dc20   96–18069
                                                              CIP

Printing number

10   9   8   7   6   5   4   3   2   1

Contents

The
Secretary's
Secret
Weapon

Chapter 1

Communication and Your Job

Let's begin with a few basic assumptions. At this moment in your career, you are a professional secretary or administrative assistant—depending on how your company defines your position or what you, personally, prefer to be called. You are employed, either full-time and salaried; part-time or as a temp; or by yourself, as an independent contractor. You obviously possess the skills necessary to qualify for your job, and you probably have most of the ones you need to actually perform it. Finally, you are ambitious, which means one of two things: you either want to grow within your present position or you hope to use it as a launching pad to the next step on your particular career ladder.

If that is a fairly accurate description of where you see yourself, read on, because this book was written for *you*. And since you are a very busy person, it will get straight to the point, give you information you can really use, and share with you the candid thoughts of many of your professional peers around the country.

The "Good Old Days"

Let's begin by taking a good hard look at what you do. No one has to tell you how much your job has changed over the past few years, especially if you've been at this for a while. The position you now hold is certainly not what it was twenty or even ten years ago. It is, in fact, evolving so quickly that many of the skills you can't seem to live without today are either just greatly enhanced versions of the ones secretaries have always needed or they are entirely new ones that didn't even exist a few years ago. If your head spins at the pace of change and the myriad things you have to learn and master in today's world, or if you sometimes yearn for a quieter, less harried time, take just a moment to recall how things *really* were not so very long ago.

Carol Green is the secretary to the vice president of Finance for one of the largest paper and paperboard companies in the United States. A veteran of twenty-four years, she insists she was stubborn enough to stay with the job because she just *knew* it had to get better. It has.

"I've seen multitudes of changes. We have gone from ditto machines and stencils and making fourteen carbon copies on a manual typewriter to the latest in computers, laser printers, copy machines, e-mail, and sending a fax through your computer. The improvements have been so great and such time-savers, and the responsibilities have broadened so much.

"When you change departments, you are changing companies. It is a constant education as you move through an organization. I don't think you can ever learn too much. Someday, it is going to help you down the line. There is going to be this wonderful job up in the sky that you are going to be perfectly suited for.

"Now I am in Finance, and I do things I had never done in the past, including a lot of technical typing and spreadsheets. We have 150 accountants. I still don't understand everything they do, but I have learned a lot from them. This is a very time-consuming and detail-oriented job. You cannot make a mistake. It has to be right. I like the numbers. I like seeing them come out right."

The secretary's "secret weapon," as you've probably guessed by now, is something very unsexy called *communication skills*. As a secretary you have always needed communication skills, of course, but never to the degree you need them now. Let's face it, in today's fast-paced, high-tech, and worldwide business environment, communication skills probably do seem a bit prosaic. Of course, if we're talking about e-mail or the Internet, perhaps they have a little more pizzazz. Still, communication skills, to most people, fall somewhere between the artistic use of white-out and the ability to brew a great pot of coffee. So, why read an entire book about them?

The reason is *change*. Consider this: The world in which we all conduct business is changing every day. Your job description is changing right along with it. And your understanding of how communication fits into that picture must also change. For one thing, the skills you need are broader and more complex than they have ever been. For another, if you develop and hone them, you are destined to succeed—whether you choose to remain in your present profession or to move on to something else. Conversely, if you fail to grasp their importance, you are stacking the deck against yourself.

➤

Elnor Hickman, CPS, has been a secretary with the Legal Assistance Foundation of Chicago for twenty-eight years. If a single word could be said to characterize those years, it is surely *change*.

"The field has changed totally. I don't know anything that is the same as it was twenty-five years ago. The number one piece of advice I would give to people already in the field, or who are aspiring to become secretaries, is this: You must be flexible and adaptable and try to remain current. It's impossible to keep up with everything, but keep up with as much as you can. For people who are coming to the profession now, it is very unlikely that you will spend twenty-eight years with any one employer. It is even possible that you will have to make some changes—lateral or otherwise—in your careers. It might even be necessary to change occupations. That is the new reality."

➤

Let's make a couple of other assumptions: If you've read this far, you believe in self-improvement and self-empowerment. You want to make a contribution to the organization for which you work, be it privately, publicly, or self-owned. You hope to grow in your job or straight out of it into a different occupation. And, you are the sort of person who takes full responsibility for your own growth and development. To do all of those things, you know you need skills; and you are willing to learn and practice those skills to achieve your personal and professional goals. If that description fits you, you are definitely in the right place. If it doesn't, well, you might give this book to a friend.

Jane Lloyd saw her job as a bridge to another career. She had been a secretary for fifteen years, several of which she spent as proprietor of her own secretarial business, called Accuracy Plus. But when Emerson Electric Co. lured her back to the corporate world, she decided to set out in a new direction.

"When I was a secretary in the corporate office, I think I knew then that I wanted to do more with my career. While it was nice to interact with a lot of people and answer the phones and be the liaison between the boss and the outside world, I wasn't satisfied with being the in-between person. I wanted to be instrumental in making changes and setting policies and actually doing something beyond making things smooth for my boss. So, I left to start my own business.

"Once I experienced working for myself, I knew I couldn't go back to being *just a secretary*. I never felt there was anything wrong with that job; it just wasn't enough for me. I wanted a little more power. I don't aspire to be president of the company. I just want to make it to director. I still have two steps to go and probably a lot of years, but I think I'll get there."

Beyond the Keyboard

Under the umbrella of communication skills fall a number of important areas that reflect the business environment of the nineties. For example, while proficiency in typing is still important, it is only half the picture in a world of computers and other forms of sophisticated technology. The *level* of your responsibilities is only one of the things that has changed; the other is their *scope*.

As an administrative assistant, you may well keep your supervisor's appointment book or calendar; act as the clearing house for all incoming calls; make travel and hotel arrangements; plan, organize, attend, and even conduct meetings; function as a liaison between your manager and other executives, departments, divisions, or companies; deal directly with vendors or suppliers; entertain visitors; write and edit everything from business correspondence to corporate publications; and represent your manager and your company to the outside world. Quite a job description, isn't it? And what does every single one of those job roles require? You guessed it—your new secret weapon—mastery of the art of communication.

In her role as executive secretary to the president and CEO of a publicly held manufacturing company, with offices throughout the United States and Europe, Nancy Butler (not her real name) doesn't care what people call her, unless her job title sets her apart in some way from her co-workers. That, she doesn't like.

"This company isn't really into titles; and they don't mean anything to me, either. Yet, while it's not an important issue, the title *secretary* doesn't really work in the context of what my job has become; *administrative assistant* seems more accurate. Also, I think, in the minds of many people, the word *secretary* defines not a profession, but a job. Professional Secretaries International (PSI) has done a fine job of elevating the perception of what the terms *secretary* or *administrative assistant* really mean."

Before we go any further, let's take a quick tour of this book, so you have a sense of what lies ahead. *The Secretary's Secret Weapon* is more of a smorgasbord than a formal sit-down dinner. In its eight chapters, it offers you an array of information, observations, suggestions, and skills; but they don't have to be selected or digested in any particular order. As a professional secretary, you know where your strengths and weaknesses lie, just as you know what you need to learn and what you already know. As you read through this chapter, certain topics may hit your hot button, while others may spark no reaction at all. That's fine. Browse . . . graze . . . even nibble, if you like. Then, fill your plate with exactly what you want, and leave the rest for another time.

The seven chapters that follow deal with areas of communication that are particularly relevant to your job. Each chapter focuses on a specific discipline, including listening, speaking, writing, using the telephone, the art of nonverbal communication, computers, and meeting skills. You will also have a chance to taste-test some of the other attributes guaranteed to set you apart from people who may share your job title but lack your special strengths.

Now that we've covered the basics, let's begin with an *attitude adjustment*. If you don't already do so, now is the time to begin thinking of yourself in new way—not as a secretary, but rather as the *front-line person*. As such, you represent your immediate manager, your department, and, indeed, your company to the world.

That world may take the form of a telephone caller . . . a visitor . . . a senior executive . . . a member of the board of directors . . . someone who reports directly to your manager . . . a fellow worker from a different department, division, or facility . . . a supplier, vendor, or salesperson . . . a competitor . . . the media . . . or the public. This is by no means an exhaustive list, but you get the idea. The first person every single one of those representatives of the world sees or talks to is *you*, and that makes your role more important than even you may realize.

➤

Teri Johnson is the first and sometimes the only person outsiders deal with when they call Transitional Care of America (TCA), a St. Louis-based corporation that owns and operates long-term health care hospitals. There isn't much difference between Teri's telephone and in-person style of greeting people: both are unfailingly warm and welcoming.

"No matter what capacity I'm operating in—a business environment or a social one—I remember the Golden Rule. To me, that means I try to treat everyone as I would like to be treated. I don't think I've ever been disappointed with the results of that approach.

Of course, there are going to be some unpleasant situations now and then. I may have a hostile caller; but if I treat that person with respect or just try to empathize, at least they feel they've been heard, which is all most people want anyway. After that, I can try to get to the core of the problem and resolve things; but this part comes first."

Listen, Listen, Listen

If any ability is underrated and neglected, it is certainly that of listening and truly *hearing* what is said. Yet, listening should be the first and most important communication skill on your list—especially in *your* job. In Chapter 2, we will explore those of your job responsibilities that require your ability to listen to and understand what others are trying to convey. We will also discuss the importance of listening; the attitude you must cultivate to become an effective listener; and a treasure chest of specific skills for listening, hearing, understanding, and retaining what others say.

Since you are usually the principal link between an outside person and your boss, you act as a conveyor of all kinds of messages. As easy as it is for messages to get lost, if you don't hear something and understand it completely, that's as good as guaranteeing it will get lost. Why is it so important to understand the message clearly?

First, if you don't have enough information, you can't ask the right questions. Second, if the person you happen to be talking to is in the wrong place—and you'd be amazed at how often *that* happens—you can guide him or her in the right direction and save everybody time in the process. And, third, whatever is being said may be an explanation or instructions you need to act on. If you don't listen and comprehend, obviously, you can't do that in a timely manner.

As an administrative assistant for a northern California office of a national search and placement firm, Cindy Eastwood talks to a lot of people who are in the job market. Sometimes they're in the right place, sometimes not. Her first task is to find out which.

"One of my responsibilities is to speak with people who call on the phone, a large number of whom are candidates seeking new positions. I listen to their needs, ask questions, and determine if their background and experience are related to the biotech or pharmaceutical industries in which our office specializes. Many of the calls I receive are from people who aren't sure of the exact nature of our business. After explaining what we do, if I can't help them or refer them to another office that can, I suggest they call our corporate office for additional information."

The most apparent communication skill is *speaking*, which includes what you say and how you say it. In Chapter 3, we will explore what effective speaking means in the context of your job. We will cover command of the English language and proper grammar, vocabulary, voice, putting ideas together and thinking on your feet, content as well as packaging, and focusing on the listener.

There is universal agreement on one point: Grammar counts. People have been known to flinch at the discordant sound of the English language being butchered before their ears. If your goal is to be understood and to communicate in a clear, concise manner, a good rule of thumb is: Think about what you want to say; and then say it in the clearest, easiest-to-understand words you can.

Mary Duda, CPS, has worked for one boss, the president and CEO of a worldwide manufacturing company, for a good part of his business life. She has also spent much of her own career learning, growing, and helping others to do the same through her work in the National Secretaries Association (NSA)—now called Professional Secretaries International (PSI).

"One of my very first bosses was a vice president of marketing. He used to say, 'You only have one chance to make a good impression, and that impression can be destroyed the minute you open your mouth.' To me, that meant you can look like a million dollars and spend practically that much on your wardrobe; but if the proper words don't come out when you speak, you're dead. I wish we could make young people understand that. Right now, I think everyone is so caught up with technology that they forget they still have to communicate in English."

Secretaries were once viewed as human conduits for business correspondence or other written material: the boss dictated something in person or into a Dictaphone; the secretary took it down in shorthand and then transcribed his or her own notes or the tape on the typewriter; the boss signed it or approved the finished product. Times have changed, and so has your role.

Bosses today are more likely to *assign* than dictate; administrative assistants are more apt to construct a written piece based on cursory instructions than on a detailed word-by-word dictation. In short, secretaries are expected to know *how to write*. Business correspondence is still important; but you can add to the list newsletters, intracompany memos, postings, and other projects.

Beth Quick-Andrews is a young entrepreneur who launched her own business—Quick Business Services, located in St. Louis, Missouri—right out of college. A born marketer, she views a command of the language as just another marketing tool.

"I think knowing and using proper English is critical to any written or spoken piece of communication, whether that is a message on someone's voice mail, a letter, or a presentation. There's nothing worse than allowing something to go out on company letterhead with a mistake that *you* don't even see as a mistake but that glares at the reader like the afternoon sun. In this job, I certainly can't make grammatical errors myself; but I can't let my clients make them, either. I have to be able to spot the mistakes other people make and know how to correct them."

As the world gets smaller, the telephone becomes ever more important for linking people together. Much of the contact you have within your organization and outside of it is by phone, and mastering the art of using the phone to its fullest potential is a vitally important communication skill. Phone skills, which will be the subject of Chapter 5, include two of those we have already covered—listening and speaking—but since the phone deprives people of actually *seeing* the person to whom they are speaking, it has a set of rules all its own. We will discuss telephone techniques and etiquette; incoming and outgoing calls; taking complete, accurate messages; handling irate callers; and screening calls, among other subjects.

Kathy Boyer is a pathology secretary at St. Joseph's Hospital in Kirkwood, Missouri. Communication has always been one of her strong suits and, in a fast-paced, five-doctor office that deals with life-and-death issues, phone skills are a must.

"I think it's a matter of attitude. Your attitude shows on the phone. If you're angry because of something that happened at home, and you bring that to work, nobody really cares. Patients want to feel that they're number one. If you communicate to them that they are number one, they'll feel much better. If you treat people the way you would like to be treated, the rewards are there. You've made a patient happier, or you made someone feel better. Phone skills are also contagious. I've noticed that our staff members and even our physicians have begun to answer the telephone differently than they used to."

Much of what transpires between two people often does not even involve the spoken or written word. Volumes are spoken through what is called *nonverbal communication*—a look, a gesture, your posture, how you handle time and space, something called *image*, and your body language. In Chapter 6, we delve into these elements and talk about how to master both the sending and receiving of nonverbal clues.

Sue St. John began her career as a receptionist, worked her way up to administrative assistant for the same company, and just kept right on going. Today, she manages a thriving, very busy medical practice.

"For me, nonverbal communication—body language and facial expressions—is often more revealing than what was actually said or written down on paper. When I first started out, I used my ability to read this language as a tool to try to stay one step ahead of what was happening. Later, as a manager charged with the responsibility of motivating and guiding my staff, it became an essential element in my job. Because I'm in a position of authority, whatever I tell my people to do, they do; but I can tell by their nonverbal cues whether they are really buying in or just capitulating. The animation in their posture or the excitement in their eyes means they buy it. When that's missing, I know I have to find another way to reach them."

One of the most dramatic changes in the secretary's job is the ubiquitous presence of the computer in an office setting. Years ago, an IBM, self-correcting Selectric was considered a prize. Today, virtually everyone has a personal computer on his or her desk, including the boss. Computer illiteracy is unacceptable; but literacy means more than being able to function in a word processing program. Secretaries and administrative assistants are also expected to be conversant with databases, spreadsheets, graphics packages, time and billing, networks, modems, client and time management programs, and more. Chapter 6 provides an overview of this very important aspect of business communication.

Jane Lloyd built a business on knowing how to use state-of-the-art hardware and software. When she re-entered the corporate world, she found new challenges awaited her.

"It is not enough to just learn word processing and be able to make a letter look gorgeous. It's not enough to create a professional-looking presentation with some tables, nice fonts, and different type sizes. It's not even enough to be able to work in a database. You also have to be able to function in a spreadsheet. A spreadsheet can keep your budget, do your accounts payable, maintain your time sheets, organize vacations, and track just about anything you want to track.

"In good programs, you can put in formulas, do all kinds of

calculations, bring your spreadsheet into word processing documents, and keep everything updated. The capabilities are phenomenal. I think, for a secretary, this is probably the most essential skill to have now. All it takes are time and training and working with it to make spreadsheets as second nature as word processing.''

With the increasing scope of their responsibilities, many administrative assistants are finding themselves assuming the role of meeting leaders. But even if you never chair a meeting, there is little doubt that you will probably plan, organize, arrange for, take notes at, and follow up on many meetings in the course of your work. Secretaries, these days, are expected to be meeting planners, public relations experts, and special event coordinators—all of which require a unique set of communication skills—which we will examine in Chapter 8.

Carol Green has worn a great many hats in the past twenty-four years. One of her favorites was that of meeting planner.

"You find secretaries doing things once considered completely out of the secretarial realm—like meeting planning. That's what happened to me when I went to the Marketing Department. Marketing, in those days, was a one-man band; and that man didn't even have a secretary. For a long time, he did everything himself; and, every year, I helped him put on the Chairman's Dinner.

"Then, when a new vice president of Marketing came in and asked me to be his secretary, I just added meetings to my responsibilities. We did all kinds of them, from small customer meetings, to sales meetings, to huge meetings like the Chairman's Dinner, to road-show meetings when we went public. It was a lot of hard work, but I just absolutely thrived on it. After a while, it wasn't even difficult. I knew all the little things to do—like going through the room before a dinner to make sure all the plates were lined up evenly. Believe it or not, I really enjoyed it.''

That is a look at the specific skills to be introduced in the rest of the book. But first, let's take a few minutes to see how they fit in the context of your present job responsibilities. We have talked a little about how the position of secretary has changed. Now, let's explore in more detail just what your job entails.

What you have read so far is that today's secretary acts as a right-hand person, an indispensable member of a very select team. As such, you must possess all of the administrative, clerical, and organizational skills that have always been job requirements, plus a great many more that reflect the changing nature of your position today. Since the rest of this book focuses primarily on communication skills, we'll turn our attention for just a few minutes to some of the other essential attributes a professional secretary should cultivate.

To function as a successful administrative assistant in today's business environment, in addition to being an excellent communicator, you would do well to add these strengths to your resume: consummate professional; self-empowered and assertive; relationship builder; and global thinker. Let's take them one at a time, beginning with what it means to be a *consummate professional*.

Mary Duda, CPS, personifies professionalism—in her personal style, her interactions with people, and her appearance. While she attributes it to her background and how she views herself and her job, she admits professional image is not an easy concept to explain.

"To me, my sense of professionalism has always been a part of me. Yet, it is hard to define. I could more easily describe how I would be if I were acting *unprofessionally*—for example, the way I might solicit information from other people. I could ask for things in a very sharp manner. I could do it all over the phone, never put anything in writing, be vague in my instructions, or neglect to say 'thank you.' That, to me, would be very unprofessional.

"I do not get politically involved. I'm sure there are politics, but I just put on my blinders because I find it nonproductive and potentially suicidal to take an active role. I have always focused on my job and what I needed to do to get the job done. That's what I get paid for—coming in and doing a good job to the best of my ability. That is also my definition of professionalism."

———————————————————————➤

Self-empowerment and *assertiveness* are more than mere buzz-words to you; they should be words to live by. Technically, self-empowerment means recognizing and tapping into the personal power you already possess. It is not something that can be bestowed upon you by another person, because personal power is an innate quality. Self-empowerment means taking responsibility and accountability for your job; feeling like a partner in achieving organizational goals; taking the initiative and risks without fear of reprisal; and, especially, willingly investing your energy in working toward results.

———————————————————————➤

Many people think of being a secretary as *paying their dues* so they can go on to something else. Cathy Boyer had her eye on a secretarial position in the medical field, but she had to pay *her* dues to get it. She did it by being proactive and self-empowered.

"I began in the medical field as a lab aide. My new boss was impressed with my secretarial skills. But we already had two secretaries, and there wasn't any need for another one. So, I did what I had to do: wear those *lovely* lab coats, set up specimens, check for 'previous,' do the filing, and all those little things I thought needed to be done that no one else wanted to do. Basically, I spent one year learning, but I didn't have enough to do.

"At my first review, I asked if I could take on more responsibility. My boss said, 'Sure.' I was in the right place at the right time. The two secretaries who were there at the beginning left. There were things I knew I could do, things I understood how to do; and I was fortunate enough to be in a situation where they let me try them to see what I could handle. I took a class in medical terminology and more or less taught myself my first year on the job."

———————————————————————➤

Self-empowerment is a wonderful concept, but in some business settings it may not be supported. There are many organizations in which empowerment—authority, power, autonomy—is, in fact, granted by management. When your boss says, "I know you have the talent and ability to handle your job. You also have the authority to do whatever you think it takes to get it done. It's OK to take risks; it's even OK to make mistakes. I'll back you all the way," you are empowered. The key to being given authority is a corresponding willingness to accept it.

Jean Downey is a senior executive secretary to the president of a division of a St. Louis-based *Fortune* 100 company. She was fortunate to have an empowering boss early in her career who gave her a great deal of autonomy; but, she admits, that made it impossible for her to work comfortably in a more authoritarian environment.

"My first boss allowed me to run the office as I wished. He traveled 90–95 percent of the time and often was not accessible. I was given the authority to make decisions, and he always backed me and accepted the decisions I made. I had a very good start in that early job, but my next boss was from a different era. He believed that women should only answer the phone, file, and offer opinions when asked. I never adjusted to that situation. I had decided to search for a new position and had a job interview scheduled for the day my present boss was named president of the company. He is a young manager with new ideas, respectful of women, and he allows me almost the same freedom I had in my first position. Needless to say, I stayed."

Perhaps no characteristic or ability is more important to a secretary than the ability to *build relationships* with other people. *Other people* includes such a laundry list of stakeholders we might as well not try to define them. In many cases, a secretary will be perceived as having authority simply by virtue of his or her association with a senior executive. But if he or she is not able to connect with people and build one-on-one relationships, that authority may soon be thwarted.

The final competency an administrative assistant needs is the ability to *think globally*, to appreciate the cultural and other differences among people—in short, to value diversity.

———————————————————————————➤

Mary Duda's scope has broadened over the years, right along with her responsibilities. Working for a company with ties all over the world, she has had to become conversant with time zones, business customs, and protocol.

"This is an international organization. When I first started working for this company, I didn't even know how to work a telex machine. So, I did some research, found new and better technology, and saved everybody money. Then, we put in an electronic mail system. That's all we do now. Being brought into the international side of things has really been broadening.

"One of the most important things I've had to learn is to understand and interact with people in other countries. We deal with the Japanese, the Irish, the Chinese, the Canadians, the Mexicans, and the Colombians. We cannot be narrow-minded. We tend to think that when we're in this country, others should do as we do; but that is not always true in business. There are cultures in which we need to learn to do things *their* way if the business is going to continue. It is simply being client-centered to do what it takes to make every person comfortable."

———————————————————————————➤

Summing Up

In this first chapter, you have been introduced to a more up-to-date *paradigm*—a new view of the job you now hold and what it really takes to do it. It is a myth, and hopefully few people still believe, that *"Anyone can be a secretary. All it takes is being able to answer the phone and type."* You have always known it takes a great deal more, including an array of communication skills most managers don't even have.

Chapter 1 has described your role as a front-line person who represents your immediate manager, your department, and your organization to the world. It has given you a preview of the seven basic communication skills this book will cover in the chapters ahead and mentioned several additional attributes you should consider indispensable to your success as a professional secretary.

That was the overview of what is to come. Now, we get down to serious skill building. Feel free to read straight through, skip around, or pick the topic you feel the greatest need to master. As you have done in this first chapter, along the way you will meet many of your professional peers who make their appearances to swap stories with you. Bon voyage and smooth sailing!

Chapter 2

Are You Listening?

If you were asked to identify the single, most important skill you need to excel in your job, you probably wouldn't say *listening*. Yet, you spend almost fifty percent of your working day taking in information that comes to you by way of the spoken word. In other words, you absorb that information by *listening* to other people say something. Research tells us that people are more influenced by what they *hear* than by what they read. As important as listening is to your effectiveness—not only in your job, but in every aspect of your life—if you're like most people, you probably received little or no training in how to do it. What's more, if you're like most people, you listen at only about one-fourth of your capacity. And, you can safely assume that even when you *try* to listen, you don't always correctly hear or understand the messages you're receiving from others.

Linda Yaniszewski is the founder and president of Executive Secretarial Services in Rochester, New York. What began as a one-person business six years ago has grown to a staff of ten, occupying four times the company's original space and billing a half-million dollars a year. Specializing in corporate overload and medical and legal transcription, the staff embodies Linda's philosophy: *Communication in general and listening in particular are crucial to our success.*

"We learned as children in school to tune people out if something wasn't of interest to us. As adults that just continues. There is a real art in learning to listen to people. In our business, it is critical. It is certainly important for me to listen in order to understand what my employees' needs really are, rather than what my *perception* of their needs is. Obviously, it's also essential that we listen to our clients. If I make a sales call to a potential customer, my goal is to find out what that person's needs are. If I find, after ten minutes, that I'm still talking, I'm not doing my job. We have to listen to get client instructions accurately. If one of my assistants takes in a project from a customer, it's easy enough to say, 'I've done his work a million times before' and just assume he or she knows what is needed. That can lead to real problems."

How seriously should you take those observations? In a word—very. In fact, when you incorrectly take in information, it could well cost you the confidence of your boss and the trust and cooperation of your co-workers. In your job, you know how serious that can be. Look at it this way: your boss's confidence in you is built on a mountain of simple, little things—things like getting dates, amounts, and phone numbers right; spelling names correctly; and following directions just as they are given to you. Good listening is so important to effective communication that no matter how difficult you may find this skill to master, *not* mastering it could prove very costly to your career.

The Art of Listening

Why don't most of us listen well? For one thing, we hear what we expect to hear and ignore input that conflicts with what we already know. For another, we tend to filter everything through our own perception of reality, personal prejudices, and experiences. A third reason is that words mean different things to different people. And the meaning we receive from the speaker may not be the meaning he or she intended to send. We also evaluate the *source* of the words we hear. That means that how well we listen depends a great deal on who is doing the talking. Finally, our listening ability hinges, to a large extent, on how we are feeling at that moment. Our physical and emotional condition, like our other filters, colors what we hear.

---➤

With an undergraduate degree in economics, Patricia Diana set off to find a job in New York. Her first position was secretarial. Five years later, she is the assistant to the executive vice president of Sales for Bridge Information Systems, Inc. She feels she still needs to enhance her skills—listening, speaking, and interpersonal—and then to find the place within her present company where she can both excel and contribute.

"People don't listen well because they're not paying attention. Listening is all about attention. It's about focusing your body and mind on the other person so you can *receive*. You cannot receive when you're giving, so you have to close your mouth. The way to uncover someone's real message is by having your attention on them and not on yourself—being in the present, not letting your mind wander. Self-concern is when you're too worried about how *you* are coming across to the other person, what they're going to think of *you*, how they're going to respond to what *you* say. Someone once told me: 'Don't just listen to the words; listen for the big picture.' To do that, you have to give your attention to the other person."

---➤

The subject of listening has been explored up one side and down the other. Experts advise everything from *listening between the lines* or *hearing the inner, hidden message,* to *listening overtly,* which means paying attention to precisely what is said and not trying to decode hidden meanings. One thing they all seem to agree on, however, is that listening well is a skill that requires concentration and effort. Did you know that you think seven times faster than you speak? So, while you're trying to listen, your mind is racing ahead. Thus, you often project your own ideas, associations, and judgments into what is being said. As a result, you can't be fully tuned in to what the other person is saying.

We also fail to listen because we feel an urgency to express our own thoughts and feelings. Don't you sometimes feel that if you could just explain yourself in a convincing manner, the other person would understand your point of view? If you do, take comfort in knowing that is a very human trait. So, by the way, is having your attention wander when you're not really interested in what the other person is talking about. That's a tough one because it seems, when that happens, your brain simply goes to sleep. One way to make sure you get interested and stay interested in a subject you care nothing about is to politely interject with a question.

When someone is talking to you and you find yourself hopelessly bored, consider this: listening covers your boredom, not to mention your other weaknesses. You can't look or sound foolish when you listen, even if you're in way over your head. Listening also gives you time to think and to consider all the information you're receiving. Then, when you finally do speak, your words will make much more sense and have a greater impact. Even though most of us feel compelled to talk, *listening*—when you learn to enjoy it—is actually less stressful than speaking.

Patricia Diana believes *being there* is an important part of listening. To her, that means not only being in the same room, but focusing her body and mind on the person who is speaking.

"I can see my boss from my desk, and it *is* possible to sort of shout to him in his office without actually getting out of my chair. Sometimes, that's necessary; but if there's an opportunity to get up and talk to him, face-to-face, I do. That creates better listening because my attention is focused on him. I do think getting your body in the same room and aligning it with that person is important. If your body is there, you'll naturally find your mind will follow; and you'll be able to pay attention. If your body's doing other things—biting your nails or just looking around—you won't concentrate as well."

Someone Is Listening—Or Should Be

What are you actually engaged in during the time that you're involved in some form of listening? You may be having a conversation with another person . . . or perhaps you're in a meeting

. . . or you are being given instructions . . . or you could be on the telephone—just to mention a few of the activities that go with your job. It may seem too obvious to mention, but there is no real communication going on unless *someone* is listening.

Often that someone is *you*. So, the question is, how do you know if you are a good listener? You may not know, but one way to find out is to ask yourself some probing questions and spend a little time honestly reflecting on your answers. There are seven of these questions, each of which is worth a little soul searching on your part. Answering them honestly requires the ability to objectively observe your own behavior and the intentions behind that behavior. If you find you're not coming up with answers, ask for feedback. *That*, of course, takes guts.

Question 1: Am I willing to learn about other people, places, and things?

Question 2: Would I really want to know my boss's opinion of my listening ability?

Question 3: Do I listen for the main ideas the other person is trying to make?

Question 4: Do I try hard not to interrupt, even when I have something important or timely to add?

Question 5: Do I squelch any impulse to complete the other person's sentences?

Question 6: Do I tune in to the speaker's feelings, as well as to his or her words?

Question 7: Do I try to get beyond my own judgmental attitudes?

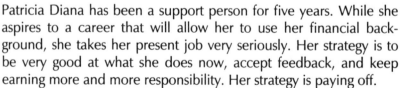

Patricia Diana has been a support person for five years. While she aspires to a career that will allow her to use her financial background, she takes her present job very seriously. Her strategy is to be very good at what she does now, accept feedback, and keep earning more and more responsibility. Her strategy is paying off.

"Feedback is hard to hear because your ego gets crushed. Believe me, I've had criticism. Once, I had a boss who said, 'You don't listen to me.' It was true. I just wanted to respond to the first task. I really didn't pay attention to the second and third things that were being asked of me. All I wanted to do was find out about and get on with the first one. I definitely took that feedback to heart. I've learned that if you're open to criticism, that's where the growth occurs."

Sharyn Lenz is the tenth-grade secretary at Lindbergh High School in St. Louis, Missouri. In that position, she is on the front lines of a very busy office, constantly interacting in person or on the phone with faculty and staff members, students, and parents. She wears many hats, including those of administrative assistant to the principal, counselor, disciplinarian, and diplomat. Every one of her roles requires the ability to listen.

"I have a very difficult time sometimes not finishing people's sentences, because I need to go on to the next question. Some people have a tendency to tell me a long story, when all I need is a specific piece of information in order to do what they want me to do. On the other hand, I tune in to people's *feelings* very well; but I don't know exactly how I do that. I guess I'm very sensitive about my own feelings, so I care about other people's feelings as well. I notice that sometimes, when people are talking, the listener has a tendency to look away or become distracted. It bothers me when somebody does that to me, so I try very hard to pay attention and make others feel that I'm really listening. I think being part of a school desegregation program has helped me to become a better person. I don't really believe that I judge people. I feel that I take them for who they are when they're standing in front of me. I don't really care whether they're black, white, male, or female."

It might surprise you to learn that good listening is *not* silently letting your boss—or anyone else—talk until he or she runs out of words or breath or both. Good listening is anything but passive; it is not only active, it is *interactive.* Your role as a listener is as important as that of the speaker. Still, as you may have discovered from your attempts to honestly answer the preceding seven questions, being a good listener requires both skills and practice. The next step is to develop some of those skills.

Here are a few pragmatic ways to improve your listening ability. The first is to show genuine interest in what your manager, co-worker, or any speaker is saying. How do you do that? By giving the conversation your full attention and involvement.

The second is to look for the unspoken meaning beneath the spoken words by noticing both the verbal messages—*what* is said—and nonverbal messages—*how* it's expressed.

The third is to let the person who is speaking talk *without* interrupting, squelching, defending, evaluating, or analyzing what is being said.

Sharyn Lenz admits that she analyzes as she listens. In fact, she says, she *must* because she has to know immediately where the conversation is headed and what she's going to do about it.

"I normally can tell, when someone is starting a conversation, where they're going with it. I have to try and analyze what they're saying as they're speaking so I can react quickly. With some people, you must react right away. You can tell by the tone of their voices that they want a response. When I talk to students I do not talk down to them, so they feel they're important and what they're telling me is important. If I talk to a teacher, I try to make that person feel that what he or she is talking about is the most important thing on my mind at that moment, because to them it is that important."

The fourth suggestion is to avoid contaminating the spoken message by verbally or nonverbally putting it down. A verbal put-down would be using sarcasm or being argumentative. A non-verbal example of negating what someone says is raising your eyebrow (if you're one of those people who can actually do that) or flashing an expression of disbelief.

The fifth is to remain aware of the nonverbal signals *you* are sending, which either encourage or impede the flow of information. Good examples are yawning, fidgeting, frowning, slumping in your chair, or looking preoccupied.

The sixth method is to try to put yourself in the other person's shoes, to empathize with his or her situation and needs at that moment.

In one of her jobs, Kathy Toennies was a sales secretary for twelve sales reps who heard what they wanted to hear. Her problem was twofold: to listen and assess what they were telling her, and to somehow get them to listen to what *she* was trying to say. Her biggest advantage was the prevailing philosophy of the company they all worked for.

"Sales reps don't listen. They just want to get their stuff done. You can tell them, 'Well, I can't get this done until Thursday,' and they don't want to hear that. I had to set priorities and tell them, 'I'm only one person, and I can only get one thing done at a time. You're going to have to accept that.' To set priorities, I had to be able to hear what they were saying and decide for myself which job was really most important. I knew what had to go out first and who had the most important clients. I was empowered to make those kinds of judgments, and when I didn't make someone else's deadline, that person's attitude was usually very humane.

"But I worked in a very positive environment—at Dale Carnegie—and they *did* practice what they preached. That was one of the best companies I ever worked for. Their attitude was so good. And, of course, I would find a way to do everything even if I had to work overtime."

The seventh and last idea is to get involved—to interact with the speaker—by encouraging the flow of information, asking questions, seeking clarification, and giving feedback on your understanding of what has been said.

While you may forget these seven suggestions after a time, here is a way to remember the essence of what they mean. Just think *EAR. E* stands for *enthusiasm* for listening—letting your boss, or any one who is speaking, know your interest in what is being said and making it easy for that person to talk. *A* stands for *attention* to the speaker—concentrating on the message, both verbal and nonverbal, identifying key points and ideas, recording important information, and playing it back for accuracy. And *R* is for *reinforcement* by feedback—asking for additional information or clarification, responding to what you've heard, and summarizing it back to ensure that you did understand it.

A Listening Attitude

But before you pat yourself on the back for being a good listener, take a moment to examine your motivation. Does it really matter *why* you listen? The answer is yes. If your reason for listening is to present a certain professional image, be aware that such an incentive may backfire. Why? Because it's not totally sincere, it doesn't usually work, and people are smarter than you think. If you become so enchanted with the impression you create as a good listener, you may actually fail to hear what the other person is telling you.

Susan Beal is the quality control manager and executive assistant to the CEO, president, and CFO of de la Cruz Companies in Miami, Florida. Growing up with parents who were both counselors, she knows the role good listening plays in the communication process. In her job, she says, it's critical.

"The right attitude is so important. The way you present yourself displays whether or not you're listening. Being able to discuss the issue afterwards often does, too. An attitude of listening means you're not interrupting, you're not bluntly disagreeing. Instead, you are trying to find out *why* the other person thinks the way he or she does. You're asking questions to verify and clarify what you've heard and to be sure you can repeat back what people said. If they say, 'Yes, that's what I meant,' then you're OK."

The next question is, *how* do you avoid getting caught up in this form-over-function trap? And the answer is that you must develop a *listening attitude* and the skills to bring it to life. While this chapter deals primarily with listening *skills*, the feelings behind those skills are just as important. You can learn and apply skills, but if they are built on shifting sands, skills can come across as more manipulative than sincere.

A *listening attitude* is one in which you sincerely attend to what the other person is saying in order to understand the meaning and the intent of his or her words. The subject may not be one you find scintillating or even completely understandable. The speaker may not even be someone you particularly like. While these things can get in the way of your attention, you *can* overcome them. If you are listening, try to do it with your full attention and all of your energy. Act like you mean it. And, in fact, *do* mean it. Try to care about what is being said. When you care, you concentrate. And when you concentrate, you begin to understand and absorb the message.

Kathy Pierce is a relative newcomer to the position of secretary, or administrative assistant—"depending on who you are talking to"—in the Arizona House of Representatives. When the legislature was in session, she reported to the chairman of a committee. During the interim (when it is out of session) she worked for the majority whip of the House. Where she will be assigned each session is never predictable but always a challenge.

"We work for elected officials. The public puts them into office. The public takes them out of office. If we don't listen well to the constituents who call in, and if we don't follow up on those calls, we won't have our jobs very long. Of course, we can't make every caller happy every time. But if someone calls in and says, 'The land across the street from me is owned by the state. It hasn't been mowed in six months, and now it's a fire hazard. What are you going to do about it?' we have to take some action. If they're upset because we didn't take care of them, you can be sure they will talk to their representative about it. It's our job to do everything we possibly can to help constituents. A lot of people call us for legal advice. We can't give them legal advice. But, if it is a legitimate complaint within the representative's district, we do all we can to resolve it for them."

An entire conversation could last less than a minute, but that doesn't make it any less important. Someone says something to you, and for as long as the exchange lasts, you should make every effort to stay focused. There is nothing worse than talking to someone who is going through the motions of listening while he or she is staring over your shoulder or glancing around the room. If you've ever experienced that, you know how annoying it can be.

———————————————————————————▶

Jean Downey has worked for a number of senior executives over the years and in those positions has learned three important aspects of the listening attitude: willing ears, an open mind, and a closed mouth.

"I learned long ago that you neither confirm nor deny anything you hear. People will question you if they think you know something they want to know or need to know. You learn to just listen and absorb and take a neutral stand. When you do that, you make them feel that you're helping them. Sometimes people just need to vent. Those are the times I just listen and don't offer advice."

———————————————————————————▶

When you have a listening attitude, you seek to understand both the meaning and intent of what is being said. You do that in three ways: the first is by asking questions; the second is by verifying your interpretation of what you heard; and the third is by identifying the speaker's purpose. The first two are closely related.

The Indispensable Tool: Questions

Questions are about the most powerful communication tool you can have for reaching out to people . . . accumulating knowledge . . . understanding both the message and intentions . . . and verifying what you heard and understood. "People—clients, employees, bosses—will be moved not by how much you know but by how much you *care*, and how you show that you care," writes author and management consultant Dorothy Leeds. *Smart questions*—which, by the way, is the title of her book—demonstrate not only your intelligence but also the depth of your attention and concern. "When you know how to ask the right questions," says Leeds, "you can make anything happen."

Why are questions so powerful? Because people love to answer them. Most of us, whether we want to admit it or not, prefer talking to listening. When you ask questions, you give others an opportunity to talk, and they respond automatically. Also, people pay more attention to a question than they do to a statement.

Sharyn Lenz fields questions all day long but not the kind she would describe as in-depth. At school, people rarely ask her what she thinks about a particular issue or what her feelings might be. Students' questions, she notes, are pretty direct—something like, "Can I have a hall pass?" And, with her immediate boss, questions often seem unnecessary.

"I have the kind of rapport with my principal that, nine times out of ten, I don't have to ask a question. I just tell her what I think. But I'm lucky because I have worked for women. I find that where a man might tend to say, 'I want this done and that done,' a woman will ask my opinion, or we will discuss a situation or a concern. Things just seem to roll more smoothly, and it feels much more like a team. I like the way my principal deals with the students. I've always felt you have to be a little bit like a parent to be a principal, so you can understand what the students are feeling."

Questions accomplish amazing things. To name a few, they can help you: persuade someone to do something . . . gather information . . . plant your ideas in someone else's mind . . . clear up fuzzy thinking . . . take the sting out of criticism . . . defuse a volatile situation . . . clarify instructions . . . solve problems . . . reduce anxiety . . . overcome objections . . . motivate people . . . decrease errors . . . open the lines of communication among people and departments . . . and put you in control of virtually any situation. Does it seem worth the effort to learn how to master the art of question asking? You'll probably agree that it does.

Let's explore a few of the things you can do if you are skilled in the use of this wonderful tool, beginning with planting ideas and persuasion. A good question establishes rapport, gives the other person the sense that you care, and provides you with a more powerful forum from which to pitch your ideas. Let's say you want to change the way something is done in your office. If you ask your boss "How do you feel this process will improve our overall efficiency?" or "Do you have some ideas on how we could strengthen this proposal?" you'll find that he or she will probably mount your argument for you and, eventually, even think the whole idea was his or her own.

Gathering information, clarifying expectations, and verifying your own understanding are three of the most obvious reasons to ask questions. When you're given an assignment, you might ask: "Is there anything else I should know before I start?" or "Can I repeat this back to you to be sure I've got it right?" or "If I have any additional questions later, can I get back to you?"

--➤

Jane Lloyd, who is using her successful secretarial career as a foundation for one in Human Resources management, credits her ability to listen for the progress she has made so far.

"If you think that just because someone is speaking to you, you actually *hear* everything being said, chances are you're wrong. But if you really want to make sure your listening skills are what they should be for your position, when your boss tells you to do something, it's a good idea to feed his instructions back to him in different words, so he knows you're clarifying what he said and what he meant. What you are saying is: 'This is what I *think* you said. Am I interpreting that correctly?'

"There is always the chance of miscommunication between people in general and between you and your boss in particular. That's why I think it's so important to clarify everything up front, especially on new or special projects."

--➤

Questions help clarify fuzzy thinking—yours or someone else's—because framing a question requires concentration on your part. "A smart question," notes Dorothy Leeds, "organizes the problem for you and for the person with whom you are speaking and offers an opportunity to find a solution."

We all know that criticism hurts, no matter how you may try to soften it. Whatever you say, the other person is likely to get defensive or be hurt. But if you ask something like, "How do you think you might improve the way you're doing this particular task?" you could soften the blow. If things aren't getting done, another question to try is this one: "What would make it easier for you to accomplish the things on your list?"

How do questions defuse a volatile situation? One way is by getting the facts out on the table. Another is by giving everyone involved a chance to vent their emotions. When a co-worker or your boss is hot under the collar, little is gained by saying something like: "Now cool off. It's not that bad." The other person thinks it *is* that bad, or he or she wouldn't be upset. On the other hand, much can be accomplished by asking a simple question like: "Can you tell me more about how you're feeling?" or observing the emotion and saying, "You seem really upset about this. Do you want to talk about it?" The same approach applies to reducing anxiety.

———————————————————————————————▶

Sue St. John has been on both sides of the desk, as a secretary and as a manager. Because she knows how it feels to be "on the carpet," she is very sensitive to her subordinates' feelings. Nothing is more effective in a tough situation, she feels, than knowing how to ask the right questions.

"One of the best ways of getting information from someone who works for you is to ask the right questions in the right way. Let's say a project is not getting done, and it's going to be late. The word processing person working on it is already dissolving from fear . . . unraveling before my eyes. She knows I'm going to talk to her. She's upset in advance. If I want to find out what's going wrong here, I have to be *very* careful about what kind of questions I ask. And before I ask any, I have to set the stage. That means taking her aside somewhere quiet, where there are no interruptions, showing my concern for her, and empathizing with her feelings. *How* I ask those questions is just as important as what the questions are. I try to use these guidelines—'Where are we now? Where do we need to be? How are we going to get there? What do you need to do? How can I help you?'—so that when we're finished, we have a plan. This is *not* the time for assigning blame; this is the time for getting the project completed."

→

Questions are a natural first step in problem solving and decision making. They make available the information everyone needs to work with. They keep the discussion focused on a solution or a decision. They help people evaluate possible options. They surface and address objections. And they certainly open the lines of communication between people.

Just applying the right questions to such other challenges as reducing anxiety, decreasing errors, overcoming objections, and motivating others naturally leads to the single, overriding result: putting *you* in control of just about any situation in which you may find yourself. If you want your boss to respect your opinions, accept your ideas, and share more responsibility with you, learn to ask smart questions. "The whole point about smart questions," explains Leeds, "is asking the *right question,* at the *right time,* of the *right person.*"

In reality, there are only two types of questions—open and closed—though you'd be amazed at how many ways you can subdivide the two if you want to get very technical. However, since we don't, let's just look at the two big ones. You ask a *closed question* when you're looking for a piece of information, confirmation of a fact, someone's attention, or closure in the conversation. Closed questions are answered with *yes* or *no,* a few words, or a sentence or two. They are very targeted and brief. They don't encourage a dissertation or a great deal of discussion.

Open questions, on the other hand, do encourage exploration and more questions. You ask an open question when you want information, opinions, observations, and feelings. Open questions allow the other person to become involved, to participate in the exchange, to think about his or her answers, and to come up with new solutions. With open questions, you gain far more than factual information. You also get a good handle on the thoughts, attitudes, and emotions that influence the other person's actions.

While questions obviously have value, you should be aware that these important tools have a downside as well. "Silly questions can make you look dumb; and smug questions, like smug statements, can make you wish you had a hole to fall through," observes author Dorothy Leeds. "And questions that make you look foolish are not nearly as bad as questions that sound unfriendly or even threatening."

Messages Sent . . . Messages Received

We mentioned earlier that the second part of developing a *listening attitude* is to use questions to check your understanding and interpretation of what you heard. Another way is to use statements that substitute for questions. There are two kinds of statements that are particularly effective at helping you do that: those that *summarize* what you heard and those that *reflect* what you observed or sensed. The first deals with information; the second with feelings.

Summarizing is a way of checking your understanding or the accuracy of what was said. While it acts as a question, it is more often an interpretation of what you think the other person said. The strength of summary statements is that they force you to go to the heart of the matter and feed back the *essence* of what you heard, *in your own words*. Their weakness is that they often deteriorate into parrot-like responses or are used indiscriminately.

Before she went to work in the Arizona legislature, Kathy Pierce was in the insurance industry and then ran her family-owned business for eight years. Going from the claims business to working with her own customers taught her how critical to success communication can be. Now, as she interacts with legislators, lobbyists, staff members, and constituents, the skills she honed in her previous professional life are serving her well.

"When I'm talking to a constituent, it is so important to get the content right. If I can take what that person has said, turn it around, and repeat it back, that is another way of proving that I really did listen. If I ask: 'Did this happen on August 24? How do you spell that last name?' I can be sure I have the information right, and the caller is reassured that I have heard him or her. Whereas, if I just say, 'I will handle this and call you next week,' the caller may not be so sure. People also want me to know how they *feel*. If I tell them, 'I understand you are frustrated. I can see how upset you are about this,' it makes them feel better to know that, *Yes, she knows I am upset. My call is not falling on deaf ears.* It seems to help people to know that I really did listen to what they had to say."

Reflecting requires careful observation of nonverbal messages—not only what is said, but the emotion behind what is said. Words, themselves, can be interpreted in many ways. It is *how* they are said that tells you what you need to know. Reflecting back is a good way of allowing the other person to vent and get past troublesome emotions and on to a more constructive track.

The third part of a listening attitude is identifying the speaker's purpose, because communication usually breaks down when speakers and listeners are at cross purposes. Here's an example of purposes not meshing. If you take the time and spend the money to attend a seminar or conference, you probably expect to come away with new information or skills. But, if the seminar leader has an entirely different purpose in mind and spends the bulk of the time being either entertaining or irrelevant, you are likely to feel pretty frustrated.

Becky Jordan is a legislator and a committee chair in the Arizona House of Representatives. She received her training for her present job as a student intern in the House, a member of the legislative staff, and a secretary to a state senator, for whom she worked for eight years. She has experienced government from both sides of the desk; and, if she has learned one lesson very well, it is how to *listen*.

"When constituents call and complain, it's very important to feed back what you're hearing. Sometimes, all they want you to do is listen. In the legislature, you never have to ask if someone's upset; they're usually upset when they call. In ten years of answering the phone, I probably had *two* complimentary calls. I was answering the phone during the impeachment (of Arizona's governor); and every time I picked it up, it was like putting hemlock in my ear. The phone calls we get are almost always reactive, rather than proactive. People tell us what they don't like but not what they would do to fix it. They call for all kinds of reasons but most often to get something off their chests. We get a *lot* of cathartic calls."

Speakers usually have one of four primary purposes for talking: to build personal relationships, to release or express emotion, to share information, or to persuade. To be an effective listener, you must be able to do two things at once: discern the speaker's purpose and adjust your listening approach to it. If you don't, and the two of you have different approaches, the communication between you is almost certain to break down.

And Your Point Is . . . ?

Let's look at these four reasons and what happens when you, as the listener, and someone else, as the speaker, are not on the same wavelength. The first, *building personal relationships,* usually takes the form of small talk or what you may think of as *chitchat*. Perhaps you view small talk as a waste of time. If you do, it's important to realize that it is probably the speaker's way of creating awareness and a sense of connection with you.

The second reason for talking is often called *cathartic* because it permits the speaker to release or express emotion, vent feelings, and share problems or frustrations. People have a real need to get things out or off their chests. When they don't, they experience everything from anger and ulcers to nervous breakdowns. At the very least, they certainly suffer strained communications. When you listen to someone who is purging emotions, you must be a caring, empathetic, nonjudgmental listener. Your job is to enter into the private world of the speaker and try to understand what that person is doing, saying, or feeling—while suspending evaluation or criticism.

The purpose you may be most familiar with is that of sharing information or ideas. *Informational listening* is probably a big part of your job. The ultimate success of informational communication depends on whether specific data has been thoroughly sent and received, correctly interpreted, effectively evaluated, and properly responded to.

A fourth purpose, which we will call *persuasive*, could involve trying to reinforce attitudes and beliefs you already have, instilling new attitudes and beliefs, or affecting behavior and actions. You are most likely subjected to this kind of communication all the time. Whether or not it works depends on your conscious or unconscious willingness to listen. Unlike cathartic listening, here you *should* be judgmental and evaluate the speaker's case before you decide whether you agree or disagree and what action you plan to take.

Kathy Pierce has first-hand experience with every conceivable reason anyone could have for speaking. As a secretary to top-ranking state legislators, she encounters them all, including the desire to persuade and influence—the bread and butter of lobbyists.

"We have contact with lobbyists only in that we know who they are. They go through us to see the representatives for appointments, and they will give us information to pass along. They do invite us to several functions. Sometimes, they tell us their viewpoints and ask us to relay them to the representatives. Sure, they try and convince us of their positions so we can pass that along. They even give us supporting documents. The representatives, who have usually dealt with the lobbyists in the past, know very well that there are two sides to every story."

One important type of listening that doesn't even require the ability to hear is *nonverbal listening.* Those who are deaf or hearing impaired *listen*—often very effectively—through their senses of sight, taste, smell, and touch. Even though many of your own choices and decisions are based on information you take in through *your* other senses, you may not realize how much you depend on total sensory listening. There is a great deal of interest in nonverbal communication—body language, facial expression, eye contact, vocal characteristics, clothing, and spatial distance—all of which we will cover from the sender's perspective in Chapter 6. In the meantime, try to be aware of how much you take in or hear through all of your other senses and intuitive interpretations.

You'll see, for instance, how often verbal and nonverbal messages actually contradict each other. When that happens, don't you usually believe what you *see* rather than what you hear? Picture this: You are talking to your boss, who insists she is listening and that you should continue. Yet, if while you're talking, she is pulling on her jacket, organizing her briefcase, and checking her watch, do you really believe she's listening? Not on your life! As your mother probably told you, "Actions speak louder than words."

Because people often tell Jane Lloyd how easy she is to read, even when she isn't talking, she has become very conscious of the nonverbal messages she sends.

"I don't think we realize sometimes how much nonverbal information we emit. Even in our verbal communication, we may not be aware of how much we convey without words. You say one thing, but you look another way, or the tone of your voice contradicts your words.

"I think you have to be very careful about your actions and whether you give off opened or closed messages. To me, the biggest sign of defensiveness is standing with your arms folded. When I see people that stand that way, I want to say: 'You are emitting the wrong image; you are giving off bad vibes; you should know better.' "

Summing Up

If you hone no other communication skill, this one alone is worth your efforts. "Seek first to understand, then to be understood," advises management guru and best-selling author Stephen Covey in *7 Habits of Highly Effective People.* It is impossible to understand if you don't master the art of listening, and it is difficult to master any art without developing the requisite skills.

There have been a number of those skills in this chapter: self-evaluation, developing a listening attitude, learning to ask smart questions, uncovering a speaker's purpose, and listening on a nonverbal level. Once you have become an effective listener, you are ready to tackle the next big skill area—speaking.

Chapter 3

What You Say and How You Say It

When you think of communicating, what is the first thing that comes to mind? It's probably what you *say*, since speaking is the most obvious part of communication. So far, we have covered two subjects: the critical role communications skills play in your job as an administrative assistant and the first of those skills—*listening*. Unless someone listens, no communication is taking place. But the other side of that coin, of course, is the person who does the talking.

In this chapter, we are going to explore that most important and apparent part of the communication process. Speaking, obviously, encompasses what you say and how you say it. But it also includes many other elements—what you *don't* say . . . what your body and facial expressions convey without words . . . how you organize and present your ideas . . . the words you use . . . your command of basic English grammar . . . and how you direct your message to your listener.

Katie Olney is assistant to the president of Gordon Graham & Co., an international training and consulting company, headquartered in Seattle, Washington. With a degree in communications and a natural gift for gab, she is at her best when she's talking.

"I think a lot of what I bring to this job has to do with my personality, not something I learned in school. I'm naturally outgoing, not at all shy, and have lots of self-confidence. In college, in communication classes, I did make speeches and debated in front of people, which helped polish my skills. But I think I always had that tendency. I felt like I was horrible at math, and I hated spelling; but I could talk! It just seemed natural for me to go into communications."

→

So, speaking is more complicated, as well as much more critical, than you may have imagined. It has many dimensions, including physical and psychological ones. Most of us construct intricate obstacles that effectively prevent good, two-way communication and then find we don't have the skills we need to deconstruct them so we can understand one another. Small talk is an art to some people and a nightmare to others. Public speaking can elicit reactions all the way from an adrenaline surge to a surge of panic. Yet, in your job, you will probably have to speak in public sometime, however you feel about it.

By the time you finish this information-packed chapter, you should have a handle on all of these topics: the physical and emotional aspects of speaking; hurdles you erect in your own path; and effective ways to keep the lines of communication open, handle introductions, get conversations rolling, and deliver excellent presentations. While that may seem somewhat ambitious, remember how important speaking skills are to every single aspect of your daily responsibilities.

→

As PSI president, Elnor Hickman is called upon to do a lot of public speaking, at a variety of events, and in places all over the world. It is, she says, an acquired skill but one *anyone* can master.

"Speaking is very important . . . a very close second is writing. Our headquarters staff is available if a president needs assistance with a particular project, but I have written most of my speeches this year. One of my pet peeves—and I don't have many—is to hear a person say, 'Oh, I can't get up and speak to a group.' Public speaking is a skill, and skills are acquired. They are not innate; they are learned. I just met a member in Mississippi who said she will do all the behind-the-scenes work, but don't call on her to speak in public.

I find that incredible; in fact, the theme I have selected for this year is 'Maximizing Your Potential.' Everyone is a potentially great speaker. You have to work at it. You have to have an interest in it, or you won't work at it. Everyone can do it. Of course, some will do better than others, but that is true of anything.''

Getting Physical

Let's begin with the *physical aspects of speaking.* These are the qualities others hear, often without being aware of them as separate attributes. But, taken together, they form a package that makes people either want to listen to you or just tune you out. These qualities include your voice . . . the rate and volume at which you talk . . . how well you project . . . your pitch and expressiveness . . . pronunciation . . . speech patterns . . . and the verbal idiosyncrasies *you* never hear but that can drive listeners up a wall. Every human voice is a unique arrangement of all of these characteristics. Your job, as a speaker, is to be aware of your own traits and combine them in a way that facilitates listening and understanding.

The normal *rate* of conversational speaking is about 150 to 180 words per minute. The rate at which you speak determines whether others will stay with you and follow what you're saying or drift off into their own reverie. If you are racing to keep up with the pace of your own thoughts, you may well lose your listener. On the other hand, if you process every word or just naturally speak slowly, the other person may either lose interest or succumb to an irresistible urge to finish your sentences for you.

We rarely think about our *volume* unless it's too loud or too soft. In the first case, it's disturbing to the ear, and you may notice people taking a step back when you speak. In the second case, they will have to strain to hear you, ask you to repeat, miss the point, or just stop trying because it's too much work.

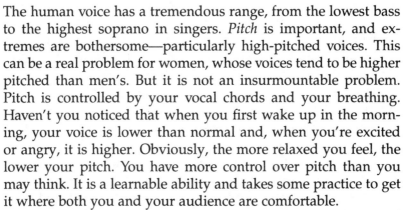

Patricia Diana's desk is in a cubicle where anyone can hear what she's saying or drop by unannounced for an impromptu visit. In this environment, she is conscious not only of her own privacy but of the privacy of her co-workers.

"Volume is key in this office. Other people are trying to work around you. They may be concentrating on something, in a meeting, or on the phone. If you're too loud, that's distracting. There's no question that people overhear you, and they're not always the people you want to overhear you. Sometimes people will chime in when they weren't even part of the conversation. I am in an open area. The bosses' doors are all open, unless they're involved in private conversation or a meeting. Basically, everyone has exposure to everyone else."

The human voice has a tremendous range, from the lowest bass to the highest soprano in singers. *Pitch* is important, and extremes are bothersome—particularly high-pitched voices. This can be a real problem for women, whose voices tend to be higher pitched than men's. But it is not an insurmountable problem. Pitch is controlled by your vocal chords and your breathing. Haven't you noticed that when you first wake up in the morning, your voice is lower than normal and, when you're excited or angry, it is higher. Obviously, the more relaxed you feel, the lower your pitch. You have more control over pitch than you may think. It is a learnable ability and takes some practice to get it where both you and your audience are comfortable.

Expression is more psychological than physical. You could have a perfect rate, volume, and pitch and still bore your listener to death because your delivery is flat or expressionless. Speaking requires pacing, variety, and inner enthusiasm. There are, of course, ways to achieve interest, such as varying your pitch, speed, or volume to appropriately convey your meaning. But the real secret is being interested in what you are saying and projecting that interest. When you're turned on, your voice just naturally reflects that feeling.

You didn't invent your *speech patterns*. You learned them

from others—family, teachers, friends—and unconsciously adopted them as your own. Some people are particularly adept at picking up the nuances of other people's patterns or accents. When you come back from a trip to another region of the country, do you ever find yourself suddenly spouting a southern drawl or a New York accent? If so, you may be one of those people. The trick here is to be *aware* of your patterns. You can only do that by listening to yourself. One way is to tape your conversations or presentations; another is to simply develop an observant ear and catch yourself in the act of speaking.

➤

Susan Beal is Colombian-born and trilingual, speaking English and Spanish fluently and Portuguese somewhat less. In Miami, she observes, being able to speak Spanish is a real advantage, especially in a working environment where there are more Spanish-speaking than English-speaking employees.

"We are fairly mixed in terms of Latins and Anglos. Latins have a whole different way of communicating. They use their arms and hands a great deal. They are extremely expressive. Their pitch is higher. So is their volume. In contrast, Anglos tend to have a lower volume and speak slower. Of course, that's generalizing . . . it's not necessarily always true. Here, everyone knows how to deal with these differences. In Miami, you become accustomed to them, and you know the people you're working with."

➤

If you know anyone who punctuates every sentence with a phrase like, "You know . . ." or "Do ya know what I mean?" or "I'm like . . . ," you have encountered the *verbal idiosyncrasy*. You probably want to scream, "Of course, I know what you mean. You just told me." But as you politely restrain yourself, perhaps you wonder if *you* have some of those awful habits of speech. You may, and the only way to know is, again, by listening to yourself or by asking someone for feedback. Only awareness can help you rid yourself of an annoying verbal tic.

Filler words are another kind of verbal idiosyncrasy. *Umm . . . ah . . . well . . . let me see* are like bookmarks to hold your place or give you time to think. In that way, they are useful; but, as you know when you're the listener, they are also annoying and create a sense of a lack of confidence on the speaker's part. Like other habits of speech, you have to be aware of this one before you can even make an attempt to change it. Once you are, practice thinking before you speak—either before you begin the conversation or a split second before each sentence, if you can develop that knack. For visual people, a useful trick is to pretend you're reading off of your eyelids as you talk. Or, if you're more audial than visual, practice *hearing* your words just before you actually say them out loud.

Besides too high a pitch, there are other qualities in our voices that can be grating. One is *nasality*—talking through the nose instead of the mouth. Nasal voices just don't sound very pleasant to the ear and are often the result of tension in the tongue and mouth. If your jaw is clenched, the sound will only have one way to come out—through your nose instead of your mouth. It comes out sounding something like a whine, which, as you can imagine, doesn't exactly inspire respect. The cure? Just relax your jaw, take a deep breath, and open your mouth when you speak.

Breathing is so important to speech. In order to produce clear, strong sounds, you have to breathe correctly. That means breathing deeply, filling your stomach first and your lungs second. Then, as you exhale, your diaphragm will push the air up and out, and your chest will contract. If you relax and take deep breaths, enough air will pass over your vocal chords to produce the kind of sound you want. Volume and pleasant pitch are the direct result of proper breathing—not of forcing air through tight vocal chords.

Psychologically Speaking

The physical aspects of speech are only one side of the coin; the other side is *psychological*. It includes your choice of words and how you use them, hedging phrases, overly dramatic adjectives, self-deprecating statements, and tag questions or rising inflection at the end of your sentences that make them sound more like questions than statements. Let's take these one at a time:

▸ *Vocabulary* counts—often in your favor, but sometimes to your detriment. Your choice of words and how you use them are learnable skills. Listen to people you consider articulate, and ask yourself what words they are using and how they are combining those words.

▸ *Hedging phrases* sound like this: "I'd sort of like to go" . . . instead of "Yes, I'll go," or "This is kind of the way we usually do it" . . . rather than "This is our procedure." They are wishy-washy, indecisive, and a good indication that you are too.

▸ *Adjectives* describe things; exaggerated adjectives over-describe. *Pretty* or *lovely* are adjectives. So are *divine, exquisite,* and *breathtaking.* Let's be honest. Very few things are divine, exquisite, or breathtaking. If something is, fine; use the best word to describe it. But avoid words like *ravishing, stunning,* or *gorgeous* if *attractive* is a more accurate description.

▸ *Self-deprecating statements* are the ones you use to put yourself down. They are self-effacing, diminishing, and erosive. Have you ever heard yourself saying: "Well, I don't know if this is important or not, but . . ." or, "One tiny suggestion you might want to consider is . . ." or, "Maybe it's only me, but. . . ." If they sound even vaguely familiar, think of a way you could phrase them differently or, even better, eliminate them completely. Self-deprecating statements are introductory phrases that negate whatever it is you're going to say. So, get rid of them.

▸ *Tag questions* ask permission. Instead of "Let's go," turning it into "Let's go, OK?" puts the decision in someone else's hands. Making sentences into questions by having your voice go up at the end of a sentence is something teenagers do. Chances are good it's just a bad habit and one you can easily break.

Negotiating the Obstacle Course

When you consider all the things that can obstruct the flow of information and ideas, it's a wonder good communication ever takes place at all. The list of potential hurdles and booby traps you could encounter is staggering, but some idea of what they sound like is provided in several groups of examples. See how many you recognize and, perhaps more painful, how many of them you have been guilty of. As you read these, try to imagine how they *sound* rather than how they *look* on paper. Remember, these are things someone has said to you or you (we hope not) have said to someone else.

In Susan Beal's opinion, when communication breaks down between co-workers, the first casualty is trust. And when trust goes, there is a danger of everything else following in its wake.

"When people automatically assume things, they tend to make accusations. It's important to ask questions to test those assumptions. *Why* was it done that way? Maybe the person had a very good reason for doing what he or she did. That's something you can't know until you ask. If you use questions when you're trying to find solutions, you'll be able to solve problems a lot easier. Barriers, like jumping to conclusions and making accusations, tend to cut trust and productivity. People become less willing to give that little extra. They will think, 'Maybe someone won't like this, so forget it. I'm not even going to try.' In a work relationship, you need to be able to trust each other, to help each other out. And if you don't have communication, you'll never be able to build that trust."

This first group of examples is used freely by those who feel a need to take charge and run the show, no matter what show it is or who gets run over in the process. This person creates an obstacle course made up of:

▸ *Blame and judgment*—"You've made a real mess of things, haven't you?" . . . "This is entirely your fault." . . . "Boy, that was the worst possible way you could have handled this situation." Add to those words the critical tone of voice that probably accompanied them, and you can see how damaging they can be.

▶ *Threats*—"You'd better not, if you know what's good for you!" . . . "If you don't do it this way, you are in big trouble." . . . "I am telling you to stop now—or else!" Again, the words are bad enough; but, coupled with tough delivery, their abusive nature is multiplied many times.

▶ *Moralizing or dispensing advice* at the worst possible time, not to mention in the most patronizing of tones—"You should have known better, dear." . . . "I'm really disappointed in you." . . . "Let me tell you how to do it right next time."

▶ *Arguing, deriding, or diagnosing*—"You are wrong; that's all there is to it." . . . "You don't know what you're talking about!" . . . "You know, you have a lot of hang-ups. You're really insecure, aren't you?"

▶ *Interrogation*—The tone is clipped and terse, the words accusatory. "Who authorized this? When? Did you tell him to check with me first? Why not? Are you trying to undermine my authority?"

If those obstacles are intimidating, the next few are frustrating. And they are the kinds of things you are likely to hear from someone who will do anything to avoid taking responsibility or being conspicuous. This person doesn't want to communicate and prevents you from doing so through:

▶ *Denial and evasion*—"There's nothing to talk about." . . . "No one can do anything about it." . . . "It doesn't really matter anyway." . . . "Just forget it."

▶ *Indifference*—"Who cares?" . . . "What difference does it make?" . . . "It's irrelevant to the issue."

▶ *Withdrawal and avoidance*—"You'll have to talk to somebody else about this." . . . "It's not my job." . . . "I'm sorry; I'm just too busy to help you."

The last group of examples may sound more like Band-Aids and niceties than obstacles. But that's why they are particularly effective in derailing real communication. Someone who wants everyone to feel good and be happy will use any ploy to make it happen, including:

▸ *The silver-lining approach* (cheerful): "It will all work out for the best, believe me." . . . "Don't worry, you can handle this." . . . "Now, now, don't be upset over this; It's just not worth it."

▸ *Self-depreciation* (almost whining): "This is all my fault." . . . "How could I have done anything that stupid?" . . . "I'm so sorry."

▸ *Digression* (conspiratorial): "If you think you've got problems, let me tell you what happened to me." . . . "Oh, heck, let's just go out for lunch and talk about something more pleasant."

▸ *Easy compromises*: "There's no reason to argue over such a little thing." . . . "It doesn't matter to me. We'll do it your way."

With all the ways to trip up yourself or the other person, how could you ever hope to keep the lines of communication open? There *is* a way to negotiate the tricky obstacle course we've just described. In fact, there are five ways. They are: being aware of how you communicate now, maintaining a two-way flow of information, getting your message across clearly, learning to process, and establishing trust.

Let's start with knowing how you communicate right now. Like some of the questions we posed in the last chapter on listening skills, this kind of introspection isn't easy. Even when you look back on your experience, you may have some difficulty assessing your own communication style. One way to find out how you communicate is to ask other people for feedback.

Maintaining a two-way flow of information ideas and feelings helps to get and keep both you and the other person involved and talking. Begin with listening at a *thinking* level, which means really hearing what the other person says. That's why we covered listening first—because it's so important. When you listen at a thinking level, you *summarize* what you've heard and *reflect* what you have observed and sensed.

You also keep both people in the conversation, making it a dialogue, not a monologue. You demonstrate that you're interested in what the other person is saying and that you understand both its content and its purpose. Next, you make sure the other person really wants to talk. If not, you're wasting your time and would be better off postponing the whole conversation.

And, finally, you only offer advice if and when it is requested—and then sparingly. Those, in a nutshell, are the ways to maintain a two-way flow of information.

Patricia Diana is blessed with a pleasant phone voice, but she doesn't take it for granted. She gives a lot of thought to her content and her delivery. The *how*, she insists, matters as much as the *what*.

"*How* you say something is really critical. You really do have to be sensitive to your delivery. If you are talking to a client, you want to project the best impression possible. On the phone, give the caller 100 percent of the information requested; and say it in the most pleasant way you can. Don't bring your mood or personal life into the conversation. If you don't know something, be honest. Don't be shy about admitting you don't know. Just say you will find someone else who does know. Don't overwhelm callers with more information than they need. Instead, give them what they want in the shortest amount of time, and ask if there's anything else you can provide. Then *let them speak*. There is no formula for this. It's more of an art form, a personal skill."

The third way to dismantle the obstacles is to get across what you're trying to say in the clearest, most efficient way possible. To accomplish this, start by using the right words. Say what you mean. Space your ideas. And be alert to differences in interpretation. If you did *only* those things, can you imagine how well at least *your* side of any conversation would go?

Learning to process is a good way to create a problem-solving climate that is relatively free of the obstacles described earlier. Process skills help two people in a conversation confront and resolve problems in two ways: first, by using first-person or *I* statements whenever you can; and, second, by zeroing in on the communication process itself. If you reread some of the examples covered earlier, you'll see that many of the sentences start with the word *you* . . . "*You* shouldn't say things like that." . . . "*You* did or didn't do this." . . . "*You* are wrong."

They all seem to suggest that something about the *other* person's behavior should be changed. They all find fault. On the other hand, when you start a sentence with the word *I*, instead of *you*, you're taking responsibility for your own thoughts and feelings. Instead of saying, *"You're* taking too long," or *"You've* bungled this job again," you might say, *"I'm* feeling frustrated because this job has been done three times now. Frankly, this is getting expensive, and *I* don't know what to do about it."

Becky Jordan and her former boss, an Arizona state senator, spent considerable time at the end of the workday, going over what happened in caucus, what happened in committee, and the general lay of the legislative land. As his secretary, Jordan was in a unique position to understand and articulate the senator's views and to speak on his behalf when necessary.

"I never really spoke for him, but I always knew what he was going to say. I understood his position, even on issues we didn't agree on. If you're a personal secretary and your boss gives you a lot of responsibility and the independence to operate the office, I think the time you can spend together bringing each other up to date is critical.

"Now that I'm on the other side of the table, I know how important it is that we let our secretaries know what our positions are, so they can tell other people. That way, every phone call doesn't have to be returned; and it's much more efficient for your secretary to answer the questions. She is on the front line. She is the interface between the legislator and our constituents. A secretary can make or break you with your district."

Focusing on the *process* means saying, in effect, "Something seems to have gone wrong with the way we are communicating. Let's see if we can figure out what it is and fix it." The problem, if there is one, belongs to both of you. It is nobody's fault—certainly not the other person's. Rather, it is a breakdown in the process, which, *together*, you can fix.

The fifth and final way to dismantle barriers is by establishing trust. If your behavior or demeanor is viewed as phony or manipulative, your chances of being heard, believed, or accepted are very poor. The rules here are: don't score points at the other person's expense . . . do create an environment where people can talk and seek solutions, not place blame . . . do focus on the objective facts and stay away from personalities . . . and do go for a win-win outcome whenever possible.

Carol Green views open communication as an essential ingredient in any smoothly run office but observes that not everyone shares that philosophy. "Communication is our business," she says. "It's also our biggest stumbling block.

"Lack of communication is one of the biggest problems between secretaries and their immediate bosses and co-workers. A lot of people do *not* like to share information. Maybe, for some people, it's a power issue. Even in small departments, you can get busy and not communicate with each other. That affects the department as a whole. At one time, when we had the luxury of a little more time, we had weekly staff meetings. They took about an hour a week, but it was well worth it. Sometimes that was the only time we had to talk to each other."

OK, now you are armed with skills. The big question is, how will you use them? In this last part of Chapter 3, we're going to go from one extreme to the other—from making small talk with one other person to making presentations to many people. Both, believe it or not, are very difficult for many people; but both can also make the critical difference in your career. Let's start small with an ability that gets a bad rap precisely because it is small.

Small *Can* Be Beautiful

Small talk is hard to take seriously. Yet, when two people are up for a promotion and their technical skills are just about the same, who do you think will get it? The answer is the person with superior people skills. The highly respected Stanford Research

Institute, Harvard University, and Carnegie Foundation all report that technical skills and knowledge account for only 15 percent of the reason you get a job, keep your job, or move up in
your job. Eighty-five percent of your job success has to do with
your people skills. The ability to make small talk work for you
is one of those skills.

Cindy Eastwood never thought of small talk as one of her strengths.
She admits she does better on the phone than face-to-face, but
thinks of what she does as *keeping people company* while they're
waiting.

"I don't spend a lot of time talking to each client who calls
unless I know their account executive is tied up on another line.
Some clients are very hard to reach on the phone, so I try to keep
the person occupied instead of putting him on hold or taking a message. We discuss all kinds of subjects . . . the weather, family, trips
they've taken, and sometimes the candidate (if I have gotten to
know the client, and we have spoken before). This gives the account
executive a chance to complete his or her call. Some clients, however, only want to leave a message if the account executive cannot
take their call right away."

"Whether you love it or hate it, have the gift of gab, or just fake
it, success depends on being able to make the most of all your
contacts," say management consultants and authors Anne Baber
and Lynne Waymon in their book *Great Connections: Small Talk
and Networking for Business.* Considered the number one skill in
business today is the ability to communicate a message to
strangers. And while small talk is unappreciated and undervalued, it is also inescapable in everyday life and in business circles.
Rule number one for small talk, insist Baber and Waymon, is
take it seriously.

Rule number two is enjoy yourself. Enjoying a conversation
has less to do with the subject matter than with your attitude.
Enjoying yourself involves commitment—to the person you are
talking to, to the moment you are in, and to the discovery of

some common ground shared by both of you. You probably know people who are so focused on themselves that their conversations are really monologues. Put two of them together, and they are like toddlers digging side by side in a sandbox—each playing alone.

To make a satisfying contact with others, you have to *want* to make a connection. Why would you want to do that? For one thing, if you see people as walking encyclopedias or how-to books, you can learn just about anything from them by simply asking questions. For another, every conversation is an opportunity, even if you may not see it at the moment. Here are a few more reasons: Small talk can help you explore today's world and look into the future, discover trends and uncover people's unmet needs and wants, find a potential friend, stumble on an opportunity, and broaden your perspective.

The moment of introduction is one of the most important moments in a relationship. However you have handled introductions in the past, try this approach next time. Listen to the other person's name, shake hands, look him or her in the eye, repeat the name, and savor it. Yes, *savor* it. No kidding. Then try these eight little tricks:

1. Slow down. Deliberately take the time to do more than merely exchange names. Say something, even if it is only one sentence, and repeat the name at least once.
2. Look for a personal connection—perhaps someone else you know with the same name.
3. Visualize a picture to help you remember the name. Associate the name with that picture.
4. Ask the person to spell his or her name.
5. Ask the person about the name's origin or some other question about it.
6. Tell people what you have heard about them. Acknowledge each person's uniqueness.
7. Give people a way to remember *your* name.
8. Keep your energy level high. In fact, rev it up. Let your body language and tone of voice indicate that you are delighted this introduction is taking place.

One last word on introductions. Just in case you'll feel more confident knowing the rules, here is the only one you have to remember: Say the name of the higher-ranking person or the person you want to honor first. In business situations, particularly, you can't go too far wrong if you remember that.

Susan Beal thinks small talk is unavoidable in both business and social settings—something you simply *must* learn if you're going to be successful in either realm.

"In our society, everybody learns it, because you do it everywhere. In any social situation, you have to be able to talk small talk. There's no choice, especially here in this office. It's always a good idea to come in and greet everybody. I have to relate to these people every day; I see them more than I do my family."

Once you're past the introduction, what next? Next, of course, you need some ways to get a conversation rolling. Follow up on those little gifts the other person gave you—the pieces of extra information that helped you remember his or her name. Talk about what's on your mind. Reflect on the occasion, event, or activity you're both sharing. Comment on the obvious— anything you observe that you might not ordinarily mention. Notice other people, especially the person you're talking to. Acknowledge or appreciate someone else—for no reason, out of the blue—and do it out loud. Ask about origins and history.

To Patricia Diana, assistant to an executive in a market data information company, small talk is too important to be taken lightly.

"I think it shows that we're human and we're all in this together, working nine to five. I like the human element of small talk, as long as it doesn't get too personal or too detailed. I don't think it's necessary to talk about your husband or your problems. And small talk should not be flirtatious, especially in an office setting and especially with clients. Obviously, a lot of that goes on, but you're taken much more seriously if you can avoid it. If you know you flirt, try to curtail it and take it outside of the office."

One reason people shun small talk is that it can backfire. Authors Anne Baber and Lynne Waymon list ten "small talk sins" you definitely want to avoid. The first is giving too many details or making your comments so long they become monologues. Two more are bragging and interrogating. Focusing too much on yourself can be a real turnoff and, while questions are great, it's important to know when enough is enough. Insisting on one-upmanship is fourth. If the other person tells a story, don't try to top it just to make yourself look good. You'll only look bad. Seeking free advice—especially when the other person usually charges clients for that advice—qualifies as very bad taste.

Interrupting is the sixth no-no. If you never let the other person get a word in edgewise, you're not having a conversation, you're delivering a soliloquy. Refusing to play is the seventh. This one is tricky. If you're not used to talking about yourself or revealing anything personal, you may not hold up your end of the conversation, which effectively puts an end to small talk. Number eight is trying to make converts. People who have all the answers and only want to bring others around to their way of thinking are *not* making small talk. While it's fine to express your opinion, remember, you are not there to *sell* it.

Giving advice, especially unsolicited advice, is the ninth. If you evaluate your own life, you reveal yourself. But if you evaluate other people's lives, you will probably offend them. The tenth and final sin is also the biggest. It is coming across as a bigot. Jokes or comments about race, religion, gender, age, national origin, or disabilities have no place in today's diverse business world. Be sensitive, be aware, and be careful on this one.

The Four Ps of Presentations

Now we move to the other end of the spectrum, from small talk to big talk, which is how many people view giving a presentation. It seems large—larger than life, in fact. But, in some ways, it's actually easier than engaging a veritable stranger in one-on-one conversation. "Making presentations," write Arleen LaBella and Dolores Leach, coauthors of *Personal Power: The Guide for Today's Working Woman*, "is one of the best ways to build your personal power and professional impact. It gives you visibility within your organization and respect from your peers." There are four steps in public speaking that reduce presentations from terrifying to manageable and even enjoyable. Really . . . enjoyable *is* possible.

Cindy Eastwood, who works for a national search and placement firm in California, avoids making presentations. To her, there is nothing pleasant about speaking to a large group of people or even to a small group. She is much more at ease in one-on-one conversations, where, in fact, she excels.

"I am really happy with this office because it's small, and I'm not required to communicate with so many people. Others have told me I'm good at communicating, but it is not something I'm comfortable doing. This has been true throughout my career. I have never liked to get up and speak in front of a group. The only two times I've tried to do it, I've become totally 'tongue-tied.' Most of the communicating I do is over the phone, and I find I do much better on the phone than face-to-face."

The four steps to effective presentations are prepare, practice, present, and process. Let's start with *prepare*. You must begin with genuine enthusiasm for your subject. It's not enough that your message is worthwhile in *your* mind. If you want anyone else to think so, you are going to have to infuse energy, enthusiasm, conviction, and spontaneity into that message. And you can't do that if you're not excited about it. Next, give your subject some color. A series of facts or thoughts unadorned with explanation is as boring as a string of nouns with no adjectives in sight. Beyond the bare bones, you need some meat, so people can relate to what you're saying.

There is an art to speaking to every single person in the audience. No matter how many people there actually are, *your* job is to make every one of them feel like the most important person there. You can do that by preparing your presentation as if it were a conversation with one other person. Finally, visual aids can enhance your talk, or they can wreck it. If you're planning to use any, it's important that you are *very* familiar with them, whether equipment, charts, handouts, or a blackboard. Do not leave your visual aids to chance.

Next is the *practice* stage. The first time you give a presentation in public should never be the first time. Practice! Go over the actual sequence again and again. Listen to yourself on a tape recorder. If you can, videotape yourself. Practice in front of people, and ask for feedback. Visualize yourself being calm, yet excited about your message. Imagine how attentive your audience will be. Practice looking directly at your audience, focusing for ten to twenty seconds on individuals and sections of people in the room.

Think about your voice. Pace your words so you are not speaking too fast or too slowly. Breathe deeply, which will relax you and deepen the tonal quality of your voice. Use gestures and movements to add emphasis to the points you want people to remember. Gesture *during* your statements, not before or after them. Your posture makes an instant impression and influences your audience's perceptions throughout your presentation. So, wear comfortable shoes, stand forward with your weight balanced on the balls of your feet, and don't rock back and forth. And, most important, relax.

Before you begin your *presentation*, take a few moments to center yourself. The goal is to use all of your internal resources to present your own personal power and energy. Authors LaBella and Leach suggest that you find a statement, image, or feeling that captures the essence of your power. To do that, go back to a time when you felt positive, competent, loved, and good about yourself. From this relaxed, confident part of you, let a statement emerge that captures all of these positive feelings. Here are some examples: "I am well qualified to present this topic." . . . "I can do this." . . . "I am knowledgeable and want to share my knowledge with others." . . . "I am well prepared, and you will enjoy listening to me."

As production manager for Ideas To Images, an electronic prepress and print service company in St. Louis, Missouri, Kathy Toennies interacts with all levels of people all the time. For someone who thought of herself as reserved and quiet, learning to speak in front of an audience did more to prepare her for her present job than any other experience she has had.

"When I worked at Dale Carnegie, communication was the biggest thing. That's what they taught. Everyone had to go through their public speaking class. I hated it, because I hated speaking in front of people. I was afraid to stand up and say my name—I was so timid and shy. We had to give a speech every night. Sometimes, I got sick before class thinking, *I can't do this.* I was just so far out of my comfort zone. But the more I did it, the easier it got; and having all those people there to support you helps a lot.

"Taking that class was the best thing I ever did. It helped my confidence level tremendously. That was probably the number one thing I got out of it. It also affected the way I deal with clients now. Before I went through that course, I wouldn't have been able to go out with a client on a press check, which is something I do all the time now."

Every person's centering technique is unique. If you don't already have one, take time to discover this valuable resource in yourself. You'll probably find many, many other times to use it besides presentations. If you have done steps one and two, your presentation should be a piece of cake. The only element you can't control is your audience, but you *can* manage it.

Of course, we hope your audience is interested and attentive; but if you are plagued with challengers or talkers, there are diplomatic though firm ways to handle them. When someone wants to tell you and everyone else everything he or she knows, treat that person with firmness, care, respect, and acceptance. You might say: "You seem to have some experience with what

I'm talking about. I'd be happy to spend some time with you after my presentation to explore your ideas."

If the talker distracts you and your audience by chatting with a neighbor during your presentation, try moving physically toward that person to recapture his or her attention. You can also ask for questions or comments from the audience to deflect attention back to you. Annoying as problem people can be, when you find yourself confronting one, don't lose sight of that person's feelings and your own need to manage them in a constructive manner. Ask yourself, "How can I use that person's energy in a way that will benefit me and the rest of this group?"

After each presentation, it's important for you to evaluate your performance so you can learn from it. *Processing* has two steps: self-evaluation and feedback. If you do receive evaluation forms, don't look at them until you have asked yourself these questions: "What did I do today in my presentation that worked? . . . What did I do today in my presentation that did not work? . . . If I were to do the same presentation tomorrow, what would I change?"

After you have spent a little time in your own self-evaluation, ask for feedback from others. Remember that feedback is specific, based on observable data, and useful only if you think it is. In other words, *you* decide if the information you receive is of value to you. The questions you ask others who heard your presentation are similar to the ones you asked yourself: "What did I do today in my presentation that was most valuable to you? . . . What did I do today in my presentation that was least valuable to you? . . . If you were to listen to this presentation again tomorrow, what would you like to see changed?"

Successful presentations don't just happen. They are not the result of luck or innate talent. Presentation skills are learned and earned by those who prepare, practice, present, and process effectively. For the big talk subjects, don't forget the four Ps.

Summing Up

Once again, there is a great deal of information in a single chapter. If speaking is the first thing that comes to mind when you think about communicating, it's no wonder. Few things are more important, more obvious, or more complex. Under the umbrella of speaking skills, in this chapter we have explored its physical and psychological aspects, many of the ways in which effective communication can be blocked and how to dismantle those potential obstacles, rules of the road for making small talk that creates big results, and a proven four-step process for giving effective presentations. Next, we turn to a subject that intimidates even those who are pretty good at it—*writing*.

Chapter 4

The Art and Craft of Writing

What do most people find intimidating when it comes to communication? If you answered "writing," you were right. So try to stay calm as we plunge into this much maligned and often misunderstood topic. As you can see, there is a logical order to the communication skills you need to excel in your present job and grow in your career. You have now explored two of them: what it takes to listen and to speak well. Without mastery of these two competencies, you cannot hope to become an effective writer. With it, you are positioned to make full use of what you hear, understand, and wish to express.

Why Bother?

As you already know, your duties as an administrative assistant have probably changed more in this realm than in any other aspect of your work. With that in mind, there seems to be no avoiding the inevitable. You must become a competent writer!

No more are secretaries merely vehicles for their bosses' words, whatever those words may be and no matter how they are arranged. It's not hard to imagine your predecessors flinching as they took shorthand or dictation and typed up exactly what they heard, no matter how atrocious it might have been. A big part of your job now is *fixing* anything that needs fixing and often inventing it from scratch. Instead of "Take a letter . . . ," you are more likely to hear, "Please *draft* a letter. . . ." You obviously need a far more sophisticated set of skills to create and originate your own words on paper than you do to duplicate someone else's.

➤

Karen Brunner, CPRW—owner of Brunner Professional Services in Buena Park, California—provides an array of services for her clients, including writing for them and copyediting what they write.

"There are three levels of copyediting, according to the San Diego Professional Editors Network. The first, called *light*, includes correcting errors in spelling, punctuation, and grammar and fixing capitalization, numbers, and abbreviations. The second, *medium*, includes all those in light, plus eliminating sexism, tightening wording, checking for logical flaws, cross-checking references and footnotes, getting permissions, and marking design elements for the typesetter. *Heavy* copyediting incorporates all of medium, plus revising murky passages to improve clarity and changing passive to active voice. I always ask my regular clients how heavily they want me to edit.

"I compose letters for my clients all the time. They tell me what they want to say; I write it for them and fax over a proof. If it's OK, we go with it. When I'm writing for someone else, I try to capture their personality. If they use special wording or jargon, when I send the proof, they will insert it or change what I've written if it's incorrect."

➤

Business correspondence, as mentioned earlier, is now only one of the many kinds of writing you are likely to find yourself doing. While letters and memos will certainly always have an important place in your job, your newly honed writing skills must now also include newsletters, proposals, presentations, speeches, and a wide range of other written materials. In this chapter, we are going to cover: the "rules of the road" for writing well, from thinking clearly to building transitions; a two-pronged, foolproof approach to any kind of letter writing; eight beyond-the-basics guidelines for exceptional letter writing; and the specific kinds of correspondence that are likely to fall within your job responsibilities.

➤

Among Cathy Boyer's secretarial duties is digital medical transcription, in which she must not only decipher the technical terminology but five separate voice patterns as well. For two of those voices, English is a second language.

"In my present job, I work for five pathologists—one is Chinese, another Spanish speaking. Both have accents. What they do is dictate medical reports; what I do is transcribe them. The doctors' accents were a real problem at first. It was something I had to get used to. Sometimes, I play editor. I'm not changing the *diagnosis*, just the English. I try to keep the system flowing by putting in the right words, highlighting them, and jotting down a note asking, 'Here's a suggestion. Might this be the word you were looking for?' I've been typing one of the doctor's reports for two years, and I do reword a lot of what she says when I think I know what she means. She doesn't mind and, in fact, finds it helpful."

Frankly, the idea of writing *anything* scares many people half to death. Someone who is ordinarily quite coherent and articulate can literally have an anxiety attack at the very idea of committing words to paper, or computer screen, as is more likely these days. It is as if writing were accomplished in a different language than speaking, and they have not been adequately schooled in this other language.

Also, spoken English is more relaxed than written English. If you don't punctuate correctly when you talk, no one knows, or cares. But all the possibilities for error are glaringly apparent on paper, including misspelled words, misplaced commas, dangling participles, and heaven knows what else. It can be, and for most people is, very intimidating. Obviously, we can't go through an entire grammar course in a single chapter; but you should know there are many such courses available, not to mention books and a host of other resources.

Jean Downey has gone from *taking a letter* to creating correspondence in her twenty-eight-year career. Along the way she has returned to school, overcome her fear of writing, and developed a comfortable relationship with English grammar.

"Years ago, I never realized how important learning the English language was to this job. Oftentimes people think *anyone* can be a secretary, but that's not true. If you don't have good written communication skills, you'll *never* be a good secretary because what you put on paper is what people think of you. And they are quick to point out your mistakes. I didn't have much college behind me when I started in the secretarial field. I had mostly business subjects—typing and shorthand and other courses that were relevant at the time. Later, when I went back to school and took writing courses and grammar, it was so much easier; though I did struggle over every paper to make it absolutely perfect, tight, and succinct."

When All Else Fails, Look It Up

If grammar and punctuation are obstacles to your self-confidence as a writer, take a proactive approach to dismantling this needless hurdle. As a professional secretary, you need tools; and those tools are the essential books in every writer's library. At the very least, you should have a handy spelling reference (which is not the same as spell check on your word processing software); a good dictionary; and a *Roget's Thesaurus* or some other source of synonyms. No one who puts words on paper can live without these essentials. What else? A visit to any reference section of your favorite bookstore should amaze and delight you.

Consider this list of titles from the author's bookshelf, just to give you a picture of the variety of resources available to anyone who writes. This writer has within easy reach:

- *Webster's Ninth New Collegiate Dictionary*
- Mosby's *Medical Dictionary*
- Strunk and White's *The Elements of Style*
- Bartlett's *Familiar Quotations*
- *Dictionary of American Slang*
- *Words Into Type*
- *Word Abuse*
- *The Business Writer's Handbook*
- Fowler's *Modern English Usage*
- *The New York Times Stylebook*
- *2,715 One-Line Quotations for Speakers, Writers & Raconteurs*

- Funk & Wagnalls' *Modern Guide to Synonyms*
- *New York Public Library Desk Reference*
- and a dog-eared copy of *On Writing Well*, by William Zinsser

Of course, you don't need them all, but a few would equip you very well for this aspect of your work.

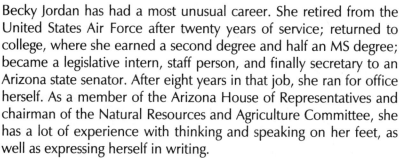

Becky Jordan has had a most unusual career. She retired from the United States Air Force after twenty years of service; returned to college, where she earned a second degree and half an MS degree; became a legislative intern, staff person, and finally secretary to an Arizona state senator. After eight years in that job, she ran for office herself. As a member of the Arizona House of Representatives and chairman of the Natural Resources and Agriculture Committee, she has a lot of experience with thinking and speaking on her feet, as well as expressing herself in writing.

"My favorite source on writing style is the *Harbrace Handbook*. It is a college handbook for punctuation and grammar. I am a very old-fashioned punctuator. I do get a kick out of the vocabulary of politics. One of my favorite examples is when someone who is trying to impress others by using a very big word, chooses the *wrong* big word. My thoughts on vocabulary are: when in doubt, use some short word you really know the meaning of."

Telling It Like It Is

Now, let's talk about writing from another perspective—how to say what you want to say, clearly, concisely, and coherently. To begin with, before you can write clearly, you have to *think* clearly. Writing, after all, is just one way of communicating your thoughts. And if your thoughts are jumbled, you can expect everything you express to be just as jumbled.

Second, writing is very revealing, and what it reveals is *you*. Eloquence, persuasiveness, superb vocabulary, and linguistic tricks may all seem desirable, but they will not mask the writer. Who you are, whether you know it or not, comes through your writing in the same way it comes through your nonverbal communication, which we will explore in a later chapter. You *are* your writing. It's that simple.

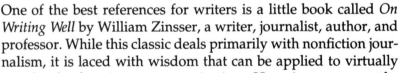

Writing is very important to Elnor Hickman. She remembers always being fond of English grammar and of having writing come naturally to her. She writes all of her own speeches, as well as a prodigious number of other projects. Occasionally, she admits to feeling a bit overwhelmed by the number of assignments she finds herself juggling.

"At this moment, I am writing about six different things; and it is driving me crazy. I am preparing my State of the Association address and welcoming remarks for an upcoming summit of delegates from around the world. I am going to Brazil in September to do a 1½-hour seminar, and I am trying to get something done on that, so I can send it to them for their brochure. I'm still writing my speech for the Northwestern Business College commencement. And that, of course, is not everything. I would tell anyone who writes: 'You are your writing. When a person reads something you have written, they draw a picture of you in their mind. So, give a lot of thought to what and how you write.' "

One of the best references for writers is a little book called *On Writing Well* by William Zinsser, a writer, journalist, author, and professor. While this classic deals primarily with nonfiction journalism, it is laced with wisdom that can be applied to virtually any kind of written communication. Here is one example. "Good writing has an aliveness that keeps the reader reading from one paragraph to the next, and it's not a question of gimmicks to personalize the author. It's a question of using the English language in a way that will achieve the greatest strength and least clutter."

What follows is a distillation of some of Zinsser's best advice, as it applies to your job as an administrative assistant. We'll talk briefly here about clutter and style, and a little later on about unity and transitions.

▶ Clutter is the disease of American writing. The secret of good writing is to strip every sentence to its cleanest components. Writing improves in direct proportion to the number of things we can keep out of it that shouldn't be there—every word that serves no function, every long word that could be a short word, every adverb that means the same thing as the verb, every passive sentence that leaves the reader unsure of who is doing what. The bottom line? Thoreau said it: "Simplify, simplify."

▶ Style in writing is like carpentry. You must know what the essential tools are and what they were designed to do. If your nails are weak, your house will collapse. If your verbs are weak and your syntax rickety, your sentences will fall apart. When you purposely try to achieve a writing *style*, you lose whatever it is that makes you special; because if you embellish too much, you simply won't sound genuine. Therefore, the fundamental rules are: Be yourself. Sell yourself. Believe in yourself. And, proceed with confidence, even if you have to create it as you go along.

Mary Hammond is a partner in a small secretarial service and building management company called Executive Assistance, located in Phoenix, Arizona. She had little to no experience in secretarial work when she bought her business, but she discovered a real knack for it—especially the parts of the job that involve writing.

"When I first started writing for attorneys, they stopped me and said, 'Wait a minute . . . there's a difference between writing a book and writing letters for us.' I think I always had a natural writing ability. I just had to begin to use it to know I had it. I think the more I saw letters come across my desk that I had to retype or edit, the more I honed my skills to pick up on individual styles. Sometimes, when I find myself taking a very hard, direct approach on certain letters, I have to stop and think, '*This is my first letter to this person. Do I really want to come across this strong at this time?*' Then, I usually rewrite it. The style I use also depends on who I'm writing the letter for—which law firm and which individual within that law firm. I once wrote a letter for a new attorney as I would have written it for a general audience. He said it was a good letter, but it just *wasn't his style.* I did it over."

━━━━━━━━━━━━━━━━━━━━━━━━━━━➤

▸ Writing is a *craft*, and like any craft, there is no excuse for losing the reader through sloppy workmanship. Relax, and say what you want to say. And since style is who you are, you only have to be true to yourself and your style will gradually emerge, growing more distinctive every day. Words are the only tools you have. Learn to use them with originality and care. Value them for their strength and diversity.

▸ In journalism there is a kind of writing that Zinsser calls *journalese*, and it is the death of freshness in any writer's style. "Journalese is a quilt of instant words patched together out of other parts of speech," writes Zinsser. Adjectives are used as nouns. Nouns become adjectives or verbs. Words just get created as needed, but they aren't really words. Its counterpart in business is *businessese*—writing replete with insider jargon. It's like speaking in code, not English, and it almost always manages to obscure the message.

━━━━━━━━━━━━━━━━━━━━━━━━━━━➤

Sharyn Lenz doesn't think her position as a secretary to a high school principal is exactly like other jobs with the same title. It's less formal, more down to earth, and very people-intensive. If she needs one skill to function, it is certainly the ability to communicate on all levels with all kinds of people.

"I deal with teachers and students and parents, and it is very much like a family. I don't go to a lot of seminars, because I don't feel I need a workshop on how to set goals or be organized. There are a lot of seminars on punctuation—on what has changed in the business world. I've heard we are not supposed to put commas after the salutation on a letter or periods after Mr. or Mrs. on an envelope. I guess I'm from the old school; I feel that the quickest is not necessarily the best way. I know that quality and a more personal touch takes a little more time, but I would rather do that than try to be more efficient. I really like to type letters and memos, and I am lucky enough to work for someone who believes in writing thank-you notes and other correspondence. Most of the other grade secretaries don't have that kind of situation."

▶ Unity is the anchor of good writing. It not only keeps the reader from straggling off in all directions, it satisfies our subconscious need for order. Another word for unity is *agreement*. Unity of person or pronouns asks: Are you writing in first person as a participant, in third person as an observer, or in second person, where you speak directly to the reader? Unity of tense asks: Are you talking about right now, the past, or what will be? Unity of mood means that *all* of the writing is casual and chatty, formal, or businesslike—not a mixture of styles. Unity implies that once you answer these questions, you stick with your decision and maintain consistency throughout your writing. In other words, you don't bounce from one to the other and throw your reader off course.

▶ Transitions are the links between paragraphs or major thoughts. They are like little bridges that take the reader from the end of one thought to the beginning of another. Take special care with the last sentence of each paragraph. It is the crucial springboard to the next paragraph.

To Linda Yaniszewski, president of Executive Secretarial Services in upstate New York, mastering the basic communication skills— listening, writing, and speaking—is fundamental to the secretarial profession.

"Writing is a big part of our job. People not only need support because they're so busy, they often want us to think for them. Certainly in terms of correspondence and memos, we try. I do some resume writing as well, which I truly love. I find it challenging and creative to interpret my clients' objectives, in terms of finding employment, onto paper. I think writing is a very important part of the job, and I am constantly taking courses and reading books to improve my writing skills."

Taking the Mystery Out of Letter Writing

When you're faced with a letter to create from scratch or from just an idea, do you just go blank? Is your first thought, *"I'm no writer,"* and your second, *"There are so many rules, I'll never get them all straight"*? If you are writing on behalf of your boss, do you worry about his or her reaction to your efforts? If you answered yes to any of these questions, please know that you are not alone. While letter writing may still be the biggest part of your job, it can also be your biggest headache. But that needn't be the case. To once and for all demystify the subject of letter writing, here are two techniques that will work every time, in every situation. The first is an *attitude*; the second, a *framework*.

Forget for a moment who is going to sign the letter. Even if it's your boss, this attitude will work. If *your* name is going on it, all the better. The attitude has three parts. The first is, be real. The second is, take a marketing approach. And the third is, be consistent. Let's talk about them one at a time.

Being real means being authentic. Don't fake it or put on an act, which is all too easy to spot on paper. Be yourself. If you're writing the letter on behalf of someone else, try to be that person. The important thing is to allow the reader to meet and connect with the writer—to establish a dialogue with a real human being. You can only do that if you remember part one and permit yourself to be real.

━━━━━━━━━━━━━━━━━━━━━━━━━━━➤

Many secretaries don't think of themselves as writers—at first. Jean Downey certainly didn't when she started her career. Yet, now she "ghostwrites" memos and correspondence for her boss, who is the president of a division of a *Fortune* 100 company. Her secret, she confides, is just "talking on paper," the way he talks.

"I never thought I could write, but I had a boss who said, 'You can speak, can't you? Well, write exactly what you would say.' So, I started composing memos. Now, of course, it's no big deal; but it used be extremely intimidating. Once I learn how my boss writes, then when I am writing something over his signature, I try to duplicate his style. Often people never know that a memo came from me and not from him. Dave has a really unique style. He's *down-to-earth*. Everybody always wants to rewrite him. When he asks someone to write a memo for him, that manager will bring it to me. I'll take one look at it and say, 'That's not Dave. That's not how he would communicate this.' Then I have to rewrite it so it does reflect how he would have said it.''

Taking a marketing approach means focusing on the reader, not on yourself or the author of the letter, if that is someone else—your boss, for example. Let's dig into that a bit. There is a tremendous difference between marketing and selling, though it's amazing how many people use those words interchangeably. When you market, you identify your customers' needs and attempt to meet them in the best and most innovative way possible. Once you know what the needs really are, you may have to invent a way to fill them. But, always, it is the *customers'* needs that drive the whole activity. When you sell, you already have a product or a service. Your job is to try to convince your customers that what you have is the best possible way to meet their needs. In other words, the product or service drives the process. While this may seem to be splitting hairs, it is a very important distinction, especially in the realm of communications.

Patricia Diana's responsibilities at Bridge Information Systems go far beyond what she views as "traditional" secretarial duties. Three of the skills she is presently using on her biggest project are writing, editing, and graphics.

"I am working on a sales manual for our national sales team. It's a total guidebook, and I am basically writing everything that everyone in the company does. We have four sales managers, so all of the account executives under those four managers will be using this manual. We are actually overhauling last year's manual and creating a whole new structure. I am involved in the writing, formatting, and creating a style. This is for internal use only. Since it doesn't go to clients, it doesn't have to look real pretty. But it does have to be very comprehensive. We want this manual to give new account execs everything they need to know about how to sell our products. It will be used on an ongoing basis and updated monthly. I'm in charge of maintaining the monthly updates. We've broken it down into chapters, and each chapter takes an enormous amount of work. This is really extensive . . . a very big project and a very slow process."

When you compose a letter from a sales perspective, your goal is to make a point, merchandise an idea, or sell yourself. The focus is on *you* and what you bring to the party, not on the reader and his or her needs. When you create a letter from a marketing perspective, on the other hand, the focus switches to the reader. Why should this person read the letter in the first place? What are his or her needs, and how can you meet those needs in the space of a few paragraphs? What are you saying that will be of value to him or her? If you aren't asking yourself those questions, you should be.

Consider this: we are all inundated with written material. Our in-boxes overfloweth. You can be pretty sure this is also true of anyone you write to in the business world. Some of what is in that in-box may be important, but much of it is not worth reading—or so the recipient concludes in the first three seconds of perusing your letter. Think about opening your own mail. The minute the writer loses you in a sea of verbiage or you get the idea that you will have to plow through a lot of "I did this . . . and I want that . . . ," don't you file it in a read-it-later pile or, worse yet, in the trash? Sad to say, but your letters may be meeting a similar fate. What to do? Remember part two: *take a marketing approach.* Focus on your reader. It will get your letter read.

Kathy Pierce has ample opportunity to focus on her readers when she is working for a legislator who thinks constituent mail is important enough to answer, but who doesn't have the time to do it personally.

"Whether or not you compose letters as a part of your job depends on who you are working for. Some of the representatives like to do their own letters. Others will give you their viewpoint on an issue and say, 'Would you please put together something for this?' I would say that more representatives than not will give you a lot of leeway on answering correspondence. They'll say, 'We have gotten twenty letters on this bill, and this is my stand on it. Can you draft something for me?' Then they will look at it and approve it before you send it out. Whether or not we respond to the twenty people who wrote us on an issue depends on the representative. Some of them don't answer their mail very readily, and others want to answer every piece of mail that comes across their desk and return every phone call they receive.''

Part three of your new attitude is *be consistent*. Chances are this particular letter is not an isolated event. Rarely do you send one piece of correspondence to someone and never communicate with that person again. So, there may have been a letter that preceded this one, or there may well be another one that follows it. Being consistent means that all of the letters you write should look and read as if they were written by the same person. There should be continuity of style and form, a congruency of person. If you took part one seriously and were truly real, you won't have much trouble being real again. That's one of the problems with *not* being real. If you have to reinvent yourself every time, it's very difficult to remember who you were last time so you can project that same image next time.

Katie Olney has been Gordon Graham's right-hand person for more than ten years. With no administrative experience, she took the job and hit the ground running. Now, when people have a question, they call her. And when they get a letter from the president, chances are Katie wrote it.

"I had never taken dictation . . . I still don't. I just sort of scribble. But I do all of Gordy's correspondence, as well as coordinate his schedule. I may have to put together proposals for a prospective client or do handouts for a conference. I put in the text; someone else does the graphics. When I write a letter for Gordy, it sounds like he wrote it. Being with him for so many years, I know without asking what he wants to say and what he would do. It's almost intuitive."

———————————————————————————————➤

That's it. You have the first secret weapon—a new attitude. Now, here is the second, *a never-fail framework*. Imagine, if you will, four empty boxes, lined up vertically down the page and connected with lines, like a very simple organization chart. All four boxes can be exactly the same size. As a matter of fact, take a blank piece of paper and draw the boxes and lines, just the way you would lay out an organization chart. This is the shape of your framework. Writing a letter of any kind, for any reason, to any person is simply a matter of filling in these four boxes.

Now, in the first box, write this phrase: *Who I am and why I'm writing*. In the second box, write: *My reader's needs*. In the third, write: *How I can meet those needs*. And in the fourth, write: *What I will do next*. These four little phrases will remind you to use a marketing approach to writing every letter.

Here are the guidelines for filling in the boxes. Remember that your reader is busy and no doubt drowning in a pile of paper. If you called this person on the phone, you wouldn't ask him or her to wait until the end of the conversation to get your name or to guess why you were calling. You would provide both pieces of information, immediately. Assume that he or she is no more inclined to guess your identity or purpose in a letter than on the phone. In the first box, *introduce yourself, make a connection* if you can, and state the purpose of your correspondence.

The second box is the key to effective marketing as well as to productive communications. It is quite simply *focusing on the reader* and not on yourself. What do you know about this person's situation, needs, desires, or expectations? What piece of information can you question, affirm, or explore? What could he or she possibly want from you that you can supply? In box number two, you are, in essence, saying, "This is how I understand your present circumstances."

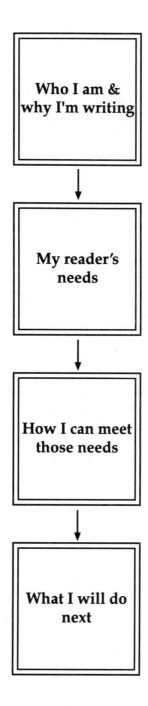

➤

While Sharyn Lenz enjoys writing letters, she doesn't get a lot of opportunity to compose from scratch. Occasionally, she writes on behalf of her boss, a tenth-grade high school principal; but most of the time, she is limited to personalizing the many form letters schools send home to parents.

"I don't write that many letters; but when I do write one for someone else, I try to make it sound like the person for whom I work. It's not that I use her terminology; I just try to make the words sound like she is saying them. When I'm writing to parents, I always personalize the letters so they don't feel like they're getting a form letter. We do send form letters; but, even on a suspension letter, I try to use the student's first name. If his name is Jonathan but he goes by Jon, I refer to him that way. I think the parents probably appreciate that we know who their son is."

➤

Why not just get into your own agenda? Because you must establish a connection at once, and there is no better way to do that than to tell your readers you know where they are coming from and what's on their minds. If you're right, you've grabbed them for the rest of the letter.

Box number three is *your turn*. This is why you are writing in the first place, but whatever you say must be couched in terms of *how it will meet the needs of the recipient. If you have identified a problem in the second box, here is where you present the solution. If you set up a scenario, here is the place for the outcome. If you have perceived a need, here is how it will be met. This is the what's-in-it-for-you* paragraph.

The last box is your *action step*. What do you plan to do about whatever you said in box number three? Will you call? If so, when? Will you do something or be somewhere or follow up in some way? This proposed action should be in the form of a statement . . . not something vague like, "I hope to hear from you soon," but a more concrete intention, such as, "I will call you on Monday, the fifth, to set up an appointment." Or, if you want the reader to do something, say so. Make your request very clear. "Please call me early next week with your response." Or,

"I would appreciate receiving a copy of the report by Wednesday, April 7th, if you can arrange that. If that date is inconvenient, please let me know as soon as you can." No mistaking either what you'll do or what you want done. And that, in a nutshell, is a workable, flexible, totally customized framework for writing any business letter you will ever have to write.

Beyond the Basics

With those two secret weapons in your arsenal, you have the basics of a business letter writing course. If you want to go beyond the basics, here are eight suggestions that can only improve your efforts:

1. *Know your objective.* Then write your letter to achieve that objective. What do you want to happen as a result of this letter? If you were the reader, would *you* understand that purpose? Would you respond to it? Don't get off track and try to accomplish multiple objectives in one letter. If you want an appointment, focus on that. If you're writing a thank-you note, don't confuse the message by asking for an appointment.

2. *Do your homework.* Ask questions, research, learn as much as you can about the person and the organization to whom you are writing. There are two good reasons: how can you demonstrate understanding of the reader's situation and needs if you have no idea what they are? And, if you didn't care enough to do your homework, why should this person care enough to want to read your letter?

3. *Organize your thoughts.* A letter is a presentation; and, as we said in the last chapter, you wouldn't make a presentation without adequate preparation. Think about what you want to say. Scribble some key ideas; or, if you prefer, fill in the boxes in some detail.

4. *Talk on paper.* Let your thoughts flow, naturally and spontaneously. *Do not edit as you write.* You can always do that later.

5. When you are really finished writing, then *edit.* Go back

and smooth out your letter so it makes sense, flows. Figure out what's wrong, and fix it. And get your ego out of the process.

6. *Keep it short and simple.* Less is better than more. Look at your own overflowing box, and remember your reader has one, too. If you properly fill in the boxes, you will naturally get to the point, write tight, and finish with a crisp action statement.

7. *Content counts.* Have something to say; and then say it, concisely and coherently. Be sure you know what you're talking about and are accurate and truthful. Bad grammar is bad enough; bad information is inexcusable.

8. *Presentation counts, too.* Presentation includes grammar, punctuation, quality of typing or printing, graphically confusing or unattractive setup, misspelled words, and all the things someone in your position should never allow to slip by.

———————————————————————————▶

Mary Hammond manages executive suites and provides administrative services to several groups of attorneys in the building. She and her partner lease office space, greet visitors, answer phones, and perform a full range of secretarial services for the tenants. A big part of her personal responsibility involves composing letters, most of which have a lot riding on them.

"*You* have to do your homework, especially if you're writing *demand* letters. You must gather a lot of information—medical background, financial estimates, ins and outs of the situation, and witnesses' testimony—before you even begin to write. The most important thing to know is *why* you're writing this letter. I would say, know your objective first, because if you don't know *why* you're writing, you won't know what homework to do.

"Organizing my thoughts is sometimes hard for me because, when I get an idea, I start writing it down. Consequently, I edit often. I would say I don't just do it once or twice but many times. The first time I read what I've written, it's for content—*what* I'm saying. Then, I go back and reread, the second time for style—*how* I'm saying it. That's all part of my editing process."

———————————————————————————▶

A Few Fine Points

If you're wondering, "Where are the nuts and bolts?" the answer is right here . . . with a caveat. Writing is a big subject for a single chapter in a very small book. Your job, as you know, is constantly expanding to include new writing assignments you may not have thought about before. Since there is no way to cover all of them in detail, these rules of the road will do the next best thing—cover all of them in a more global way. Having said that, since a big part of your responsibilities revolves around generating correspondence, here are some of the finer points on the kinds of letters you will probably be tackling.

Business correspondence is very broad; but, generally, it encompasses follow-ups, transmittals, confirmations, simple and complex requests, positive or negative responses to requests, adjustments, orders, collections, congratulations, commendations, marketing, and sympathy letters.

Follow-ups, transmittals, and confirmations are usually short letters or notes written in a very straightforward manner. A good way to begin is to compose a brief list of the points you want to cover in your correspondence. This will ensure that you don't leave out anything important, and it will help you write a more coherent letter.

▶ *Follow-up letters* gently remind the reader of some action he or she is expected to complete and encourage doing it. They ordinarily include two points: a reference to your previous correspondence or conversation on the subject and a request for action within a certain time frame. Follow-up letters should be brief and positive, never scolding or accusatory in tone.

▶ *The transmittal* serves as a cover letter for an accompanying document or item. Its main purpose is to introduce the enclosed material, or it may be intended to offer assistance or extend good wishes.

▶ *Confirmation* letters are also short and to the point. Their function is to document a conversation or provide feedback on an agreement that has already been reached. Confirmation letters should refer to the original letter, conversation, or event and clearly restate its details and arrangements.

▶ *There are two sides to requests*: the ones you make of someone else and the ones others make of you. In the first case, they can range from very simple and direct to complex and sensitive. Responses to other people's requests, on the other hand, usually take one of two forms—positive or negative—which means you will either grant the request or your won't. When you are doing the asking, state your request clearly and concisely, and explain it if you feel that's necessary. In any request letter, make it as easy as possible for the recipient to say, "yes." Certainly, avoid anything that could be construed as begging or using guilt.

▶ *Response letters* are either going to be received as good news or bad news. The positive replies provide a good opportunity to generate good will and build your corporate image. The negative replies—denials of requests—require tact and strategy. Remember, you want to keep the reader's good will at the same time you are refusing to do something he or she has requested.

▶ *Adjustment letters* usually describe a defective product or service and ask the reader to lower the price or make a refund. Thoroughly explain the circumstances involved; stay positive; and, again, make it easy to say, "yes."

▶ *Order letters* are brief and to the point, but it's important to include all of the pertinent information the person on the other end needs to properly fill your order.

▶ *Collection letters* range from subtle reminders to strongly worded intentions to take legal action. They, too, require diplomacy. You don't want to offend the recipient, but you do want to firmly get your point across.

▶ *Letters of congratulations, commendation, and sympathy* are more personal expressions of your feelings but still fall under the heading of business correspondence. They should be brief, warm, sincere, and written as soon after the event as possible.

▶ *Sales and marketing letters* fall in their own special category. They require creativity, a client-centered approach, and a hook of some kind to grab and hold the reader. If you reread the part of this chapter on taking a marketing approach to letter writing, you will have an excellent formula for laying out your sales and marketing letters. While, in some ways, they are no more difficult to write than any other kind of letter, in other ways they are unique.

Sales and marketing letters can run the gamut from conversational to promotional . . . from short and grabby to pages long and chatty . . . from a single, personalized letter to a full-scale direct-mail campaign. You may feel they are more within the purview of a promotional writer or your company's marketing department than your own; but once you get the hang of writing them, these can become the most fun and creative part of your job.

Many types of businesses require specialized correspondence, such as the *demand letters* Mary Hammond writes for her clients. Every client is different, she observes. Some will give her a rough draft; others merely a few scribbled notes. In either case, her writing ability is put to the test every day.

"A demand letter takes the case through from the very start to the end. It states the case, what happened to the client, how the incident occurred, the reason the case is now with the attorney, and the amount of money to be collected for that person. I write those from scratch. The attorneys give me bare-bones facts, and I create the letter. When I'm constructing a letter I have to be able to trust my own abilities. Some people will write out exactly what they want said; but then they'll tell me to check it for this or check it for that, fix the grammar, or do whatever I think it needs. I always have to ask myself, 'How much does this person really want me to change?' Sometimes I'll do a bare minimum. Other times, I'll do a complete rewrite, but I'll tell the person what I've done and why I've done it."

Summing Up

Of course, you realize we have just scratched the surface of a fascinating subject with our exploration of writing skills. There is always more to learn and more to try. This chapter has covered some the basic rules of good writing, including: getting rid of clutter; letting your own style shine through; honing this craft like any other; striving for unity; and building smooth transitions. From there, you were introduced to a two-pronged, never-fail approach to letter writing made up of an attitude and four empty boxes to simply fill in for each and every letter your write.

Next, you went beyond the basics to some of the finer points of letter writing and, finally, you toured the most common types of letters you might be expected to compose in your present position.

Now that you have a firm grasp of the three essential building-block skills of listening, speaking, and writing, let's move on to the fourth important communication skill—how to control the machine that usually controls you—your telephone.

Chapter 5

The Telephone: Friend or Foe?

With what single piece of equipment in your office do you have a love-hate relationship? What is your most indispensable tool and your greatest nuisance all at once? There are several possible answers, of course, but the one we have in mind is the telephone—that innocuous little piece of machinery that is *supposed* to be a tool but which often seems to run your whole life.

Linda Yaniszewski considers the telephone her "second most important tool" in terms of client interaction. She doesn't hate it, and she doesn't cringe when it rings.

"In fact, for small businesspeople," she points out, "the phone is our livelihood. A lot of our business comes from the yellow pages. When prospects call, we have a chance to develop a relationship that hopefully will bring them in to learn more about our service. I take most of the sales calls. Of course, it's not always easy to be up when you answer the phone. We all have bad days; but there is a real art to sounding up, even if you're not. And a potential customer always appreciates a pleasant, helpful response."

Up to now, we've covered the indisputable basics of communication—listening, speaking, and writing—all of which depend completely on your abilities. In this chapter, we move beyond personal skills and turn our attention to a piece of equipment. The telephone has been around for a long time; but, like all modern technology, it now does things once considered the stuff of science fiction.

So much of your job revolves around using the phone that it literally requires a unique set of communication skills to make the most of this tool. The telephone can be your nemesis or your ally. With the right skills, you can make it a practical partner in everything you do. By the time you finish this chapter you will be able to: set up your own phone center, eliminate phone tag from your life, simplify your life with voice mail, get through to anyone you want to reach, and improve your phone effectiveness whether you are the caller or the recipient of calls.

To Cathy Boyer, the Pathology Department's link with the outside world, a phone conversation is as important as a face-to-face one. While she loves to talk to people, particularly on the phone, she attributes much of her effectiveness to learning telephone *skills*.

"One of the most beneficial courses I have ever encountered was a seminar on using the telephone. These are the things that stuck in my mind: callers do not want to talk to a computer; they do not want to be put on hold; but they do want to talk to a person who knows what she's doing and won't transfer them all over the building. When you put someone on hold for just thirty seconds, it seems like an eternity to that person. Try holding your breath for thirty seconds, and see how long it is.

"I answer the phone differently now than I used to. Instead of saying, 'St. Joseph's Hospital . . . Can I help you?' now I answer it, 'St. Joseph's Hospital . . . Cathy speaking . . . *How* may I help you?' I'm receptive. I'm telling the caller, '*I'm glad you called. This is my name. Here's where I work. I want to do something for you. You just tell me what you need.*' "

A Room of Its Own

The phone is such an important aspect of your ability to communicate effectively that it's about time to give it the respect it deserves. Think about this: where, in your office, is your phone located? It is probably right in the middle of your desk, surrounded by all of the typical things one has a on a desk—papers, file folders, pens, message pads, works in progress, perhaps your in-box, and heaven knows what else. Now picture this scenario in your mind. You are involved in something. Your attention is totally focused. And the phone rings. Of course, you answer it. Of course, your concentration is interrupted. Of course, you must shift gears, which takes you a few seconds. At the same time, you are trying to tune in to what the caller is saying, you are probably also moving aside the things you've been working on and reaching for a pen and message pad. What's wrong with this picture?

Frankly, just about everything; but since it is the way you've always done things, it probably seems perfectly all right. But what if you did it all differently? What if you had a special area reserved for making and receiving phone calls—a phone location explicitly designed for this part of your job?

Why do such a thing? First, because when your entire field of vision is filled with the distractions of other projects, priorities, and people, it is extremely difficult to concentrate on anything, much less a phone call. Second, because if you have a special space for your phone, you will also develop a special mind-set to go along with it.

Next question: what would this special place look like? It should be set up as an office within an office—a phone center—that is comfortable, tidy, fully equipped, and functional.

Third question: what does *fully equipped* mean? It means your phone center puts everything you need to receive or make a phone call at your fingertips: relevant files or notes; message forms; frequently called or called-by names and phone numbers; an answering machine or voice mail system; a large, flat surface to spread out papers and work on; a comfortable place to sit; the phone of your choice; whatever enhancements you need to do your job; and, last but not least, a mirror.

Patricia Diana is organized, especially where the phone is involved. She has the closest thing to a real "phone center" one can have, and she follows most of the guidelines to make it work for her.

"I have my desk naturally set up like a phone center. There's a phone message pad right by the phone with a pen right on top of the pad. I only use that pen for the phone. I usually take my message pad with me in case a call is transferred to me when I'm away from my desk. I also have a Rolodex, a list of toll-free numbers, speed-dial numbers, and a mail-code calendar right next to my phone. I keep the whole area pretty clear, but I can get to anything I need very quickly. My desk is a U-shape; and my chair rolls, so most things are within easy reach."

A mirror? Telemarketers—those who make their living selling by phone—have made a revolutionary and profitable discovery. If you want to sell on the phone, you have to come across as warm and friendly. And, if you want to *sound* that way, you have to *look* that way. Notes phone guru and author George R. Walther in his book *Phone Power,* "Drop the notion that people can't see you when you're calling by phone. A glance in the mirror just before dialing gives me a glimpse of the face the *other guy* is about to visualize. If I look glum in the mirror, that's just how I'm going to sound."

Two more points: have your phone center facing away from people; and make sure your chair can easily roll from your main desk to your phone center quickly and easily, so you don't have to jump up and run across the room to use the phone.

Telephone Tag

Now that we have established the importance of the telephone in your job and given it a place of its own in your work space, let's turn our attention to some of the common problems this innocuous looking piece of equipment has been known to cause. One of them is that, though the phone is intended to help you connect with another party, it doesn't always live up to its own job description. In fact, of the games people play in business, *phone tag* is one of the most frustrating.

Kathy Toennies was once a receptionist, so she has been on the receiving end of many calls. As the person who now places the calls, she has some strong views on the games people play and machines they play them with.

"I don't like people who don't return calls. I also don't like the system where you don't even get a live voice. You just keep pushing buttons, but you never do speak to a human being. I think it's much better to have a person there than a machine. If I get cut off or shunted from person to person, and it happens enough, I will get angry, which is probably not the best way to handle it. When I finally get to the person I need to talk to, I will say, 'I've talked to five people before I got to you. I hope you can help me because I don't want to be transferred to anyone else.' I find that people *do* care when I say that. Unfortunately, most people become customer-service oriented only when the customer gets annoyed."

You call Ms. Jones, who isn't in, so you leave a message. Ms. Jones returns your call; but you're on the phone, so *she* leaves a message. You return her call, only to find that Ms. Jones is now in a meeting. And so goes the cycle, until one of you hits it lucky or just gives up. Not a very productive scenario but an all too familiar one, unfortunately. No one has to tell you phone tag wastes your time and everybody else's. But perhaps you didn't know you can eliminate it from your life by simply mastering a few basic techniques.

▸ The first is *learn to schedule your phone time.* Just as you plan other key tasks throughout the day, allocate time for phone calls. Get in the habit of setting aside a certain time of each day for your own outgoing calls and for the callback responses you expect from others.

▸ The second is to *make phone appointments.* Always cite a particular time of day when you will be available or when you will be taking callbacks. Be specific. If you must leave a message, rather than saying, "Please tell her I'll call back later," ask, "Would 3:00 be a convenient time to call again?" Instead of saying, "Have him give me a call when he gets back," say, "I'll be in my office between 11:00 and noon. Please have him call me then or at 3:00 this afternoon, if that's a better time for him."

▶ A third method is to *keep aware of the differences in time zones* when you're making or expecting long-distance calls. While 9:00 A.M. your time might be convenient if you're in New York, remember that it will be 6:00 A.M. in Seattle or San Francisco.

▶ Technique number four is, when you call and Ms. Jones is away from her desk, *ask to have her paged*. If she is in the building, you may be connected immediately and save a message.

▶ The fifth way is to *ask if there is another number where Ms. Jones can be reached*. If you can reach her somewhere else, do so, rather than leaving a message.

▶ Number six is *ask who handles the areas of responsibility with which you are concerned*. It may be that the person you're calling would have referred you to someone else anyway.

━━━━━━━━━━━━━━━━━━━━━━━━━━━━━━━━━━━━▶

Katie Olney initiates a lot of phone calls and obviously doesn't always get through the first time. Undeterred, she just keeps calling . . . and keeps her sense of humor in the bargain.

"I don't see telephone tag as a problem. I just keep trying until I get the person I'm calling. If I know him, I will leave a message. If I don't know him, I call back later. Certainly, there are some people who are really hard to get a hold of; and, generally, I just wait until *they* reach me. If one of those people does call, and I'm on the phone, I will interrupt the call I'm on. People are very understanding when I have to tell them I'll call them back.

"I do a lot of work by phone. We have seventy active facilitators in the California Department of Corrections—all probation and parole officers. I try to call each of them about once a month. Some of them are pretty hard to catch, so I just leave a message, saying: 'Katie with Gordy Graham's office called to say Hi. Just wanted to see how you are.' They don't have to call me back, but they can if they want to. Sometimes, they're all excited about something and just need someone to talk to about it. We have this kind of informal friendship."

━━━━━━━━━━━━━━━━━━━━━━━━━━━━━━━━━━━━▶

Musical Messages

Another way to avoid phone tag is to fully utilize your *voice mail* system, which most companies have adopted by now. If people are agreed on their dislike of phone tag, they wax eloquent about how they feel about voice mail. But, like it or not, this piece of technology is here to stay; and, as you'll see, there *are* many reasons to like it.

Voice mail is a sophisticated system of mailboxes available to hundreds or even thousands of users. It is like a large cabinet filled with very smart answering machines; but there really are no answering machines, nor tapes, involved. It works this way: the caller's voice is electronically broken down into millions of binary information bits, and the digitized voice is then stored on the computer's hard drive. When you call to retrieve your messages, the computer decodes this digital information and translates it back into an exact replica of the original spoken message.

People are frustrated with voice mail, but Linda Yaniszewski thinks it serves a real need . . . *if* you know how to use it.

"I came from the legal industry, where lawyers used to spend three, four, and five hours a day just returning calls. Some of that has been alleviated by voice mail. The key is to use it correctly. I always leave my name, number, a convenient time when I can be reached, and a detailed message about why I'm calling. When someone calls me, if I know who they are and why they called, I can do the necessary research before I return the call and save us both time."

Voice mail has a number of distinct advantages. It is available twenty-four hours a day. Callers in other time zones can always get word to you at the exact moment they wish to, wherever they are or you are. Business can be conducted during off-peak hours when phone rates are lower. And it really puts an end to phone tag. If you have a question, ask it on voice mail. The other person gets back to you with the answer and, if you're not available, simply leaves it in your voice mailbox. You can even leave a message for someone who doesn't have voice mail by putting it on your own voice mail system with a personal code for the caller. When that person calls you, he or she simply dials in a special code; and your computer plays the message.

Despite all the things it does, there are some things voice mail cannot do. One of them is put callers instantly in touch with a real human being. Nancy Butler works for a company that has a voice mail system but uses it very sparingly.

"We have a policy here that we do not use voice mail except during off-hours or in an emergency. Any customer who calls us must always get a *voice*—a live person—because we have to create that personal contact with our customer. And we look at other departments within our company as being our internal customers as well."

We live in a technological age. Voice mail is one evidence of that in your life; your PC, or personal computer, is another. It is also your right arm, so why not use it to save you time on the telephone? There is specialized phone management software and hardware on the market today that can extend the power of both your computer and your phone. PC-based phone management systems save time in many ways. In *Phone Power*, George R. Walther lists these benefits:

- ▶ Keeping track of your entire telephone directory
- ▶ Dialing phone numbers automatically
- ▶ Selecting the number where your contact is most likely to be reached
- ▶ Eliminating the possibility of a misdial
- ▶ Persistently redialing if a number is busy, permitting you to proceed with other tasks while it's busy dialing for you
- ▶ Acting as a super-sophisticated answering machine that

leaves personal messages for only the individual you designate

► Allowing you to accomplish your business and get answers to your questions without coordinating your schedule with the other people

► Speeding up the callback process so you can instantly dial any individual who has left you a message

► Sending a single message to several people through a central mailbox

► Scheduling reminders for future tasks

Katie Olney's employer, Gordon Graham & Co., doesn't use voice mail. It's too impersonal for this organization that puts people first in every situation.

"We have an answering service that picks up our calls when we're not here, so there is always a live person who takes that message. That's more personal than a machine, in our opinion. The company's guiding philosophy is to treat people with dignity and respect. We try to see people as successful. It may not be true at this moment, but we hold on to that picture of them until it is. We work with quite a few outside marketers, and we try to help and encourage all of them to succeed."

In War, You Need a Strategy

You use the phone in one of two ways: either to initiate a call to someone else or to receive a call from someone else. So far we've covered a few principles that apply to both, but now let's break down these two major uses even further. First, focus on your role as the caller—the proactive part of the equation.

If you sometimes get the feeling that any organization you dial has a single mission in life—to keep you from getting through to the person you're calling—you have a lot of company. While absolutely nothing is more frustrating or a bigger waste of time than fighting your way through a confusing, disorganized, sometimes even downright hostile telephone system, it happens every day. The good news is that you can get around it *if* you have a strategy. And your strategy should begin at the switchboard or receptionist. Switchboard operators may be real people, but sometimes we forget that. Does this ring a bell?

> **Alice:** ABC Company. Good morning.
> **You:**   Jack Robbins please.
> **Alice:** One moment please. I'll connect you.

You wait. Perhaps Jack Robbins comes on the line; perhaps not. If not, Alice returns.

> **Alice:** I'm sorry. Mr. Robbins's line is busy. Would you care
>   to hold?

[*Or*]

> **Alice:** I'm sorry. Mr. Robbins is away from his desk. Would
>   you care to leave a message?

This scenario, though standard, is actually one of the better ones. At least you didn't get transferred all over the building or get caught in a computerized answering system that asked you to push buttons for questions you didn't have or departments you didn't want. But even here, you and Alice haven't had much of a personal exchange. It's all rote, like a well-rehearsed script.

Consider this: it *is* possible to actually speak to Alice. You *can* regard this person not as an automaton but as a valuable source of information. You can talk to her in a friendly, person-to-person manner and ask for the information you need. Of course, you know that Alice is going to be interrupted frequently; but you can get around that, too. Here is how author George Walther suggests you handle such a situation.

Begin by saying: "I know you're very busy, so feel free to put me on hold whenever you need to. I'll be happy to wait."

Then, ask whatever it is that you want to know. There are endless possibilities here: "Who is the person responsible for purchasing supplies?" . . . "Who does that person report to?"

. . . "How is that name pronounced and spelled?" . . . "What is his or her secretary's name?" . . . "Does he or she usually come in early or stay late?" . . . "What is the best time to contact that department?"

Obviously, you won't always find a helpful switchboard operator; but if you apply step one of this strategy, you are far more likely to than if you just read the same old, tired, predictable script.

Linda Yaniszewski feels that receptionists have never been fully appreciated for the contributions they make. At her company, Executive Secretarial Services, the receptionist is a very important person. He or she is expected to look like a professional and act like a professional. Linda and her management team make it a point to remind their "front-line person" of how important he or she is and to pass along positive feedback from clients at every opportunity.

"We probably get over 600 calls a day. That's a lot of calls. It's a long day and a very stressful job. I give our own receptionist all the credit in the world. She is wondrously patient, which you have to be because people can be extremely rude. I think that's a real skill and a difficult one to find. It has a lot to do with personality; and, unfortunately, an hour interview is not a real good window into an applicant's personality. I'm learning, as an employer, that a resume can say a lot of things; but often it's not until you see someone in action that you know who you have hired. The majority of time we hire temp-to-perms from agencies for just that reason. I hired a receptionist once; and the second day she was here, I happened to be cutting through the lobby. She was tearing her hair out, and I heard her say, 'I can't stand these phones!' I called the agency and said, 'There's something wrong with this picture.' "

The next rung on your strategy ladder is getting to know the secretary of the person you're trying to reach—someone with whom you should certainly be able to relate. No one knows better than you do that the secretary's job is *not* to make everyone's life difficult or to stand guard at the entrance to the moat and drawbridge that protects the boss. His or her job, like yours, is to help the boss sort out those calls that are important from those that are not and to screen out all the others. This person is really your ally, as you are the ally of everyone who calls your boss. Both of you have the same ultimate goal: to provide a benefit of some kind for the same person. Together, you should be able to figure out the best way to accomplish that goal.

Another thing you well know is that the secretary deserves your respect, both because this person is a professional and because only with his or her help can you get your job done. Without it you may not. So, begin with an attitude of consideration. Do what is necessary to establish contact and rapport. Call secretaries by their names. Remember their voices. Make a few notes about what transpires between the two of you. Say something nice about the way the secretary handles your call. Is that phoney or manipulative? It's all in your attitude.

"Every time I comment positively on someone's telephone technique," writes George Walther, "four things happen . . . sometimes five. I feel good . . . the other person feels good . . . I help the supervisor by providing feedback . . . I stay focused on what I like . . . and, sometimes, something neat and unexpected happens."

The third step in your strategy is this: be brief, succinct, concise, and economical with words. Don't those all mean the same thing? You bet. Give the secretary only enough information to convey what is absolutely necessary and to whet the manager's appetite. Use benefits. Be specific about those benefits. Explain how the boss will come out ahead, why it is to his or her advantage to speak to you. And then keep focused on your objective: you want to talk to that person either now or during a specific, confirmed appointment for a later time.

Phone Time: In a Class by Itself

According to quantum physics, time is not the orderly, predictable, irrefutable march of seconds and minutes we have always believed it to be. Einstein smashed the theory of linear time to smithereens, leaving us to ponder anew why time flies when we're having fun and drags on interminably when we are bored or unhappy. Phone time is like no other kind of time; it is a time consumer, a time eater, and often a complete time waster. If you want to get on someone's bad side, the surest way is to take up too much time on the phone.

A national survey of telephone professionals who spend more than fifty percent of their workdays on the phone revealed clear agreement on one point: Time waste is *the* major problem. The number one piece of advice these respondents offer people who call others at work or at home is, "Get to the point. Clearly state your problem and your needs. Identify yourself and company. Get on with it!"

Katie Olney's boss is on the road more than he's in town. Most of her contacts—independent marketers of the Gordon Graham & Co.'s programs, in-house facilitators, clients—aren't in Seattle either. Her lifeline to the world is the phone, and she has mastered its use.

"Gordy and I do a lot of things over the telephone. We have for years. He calls in several times a day, and I go over everything that's happening in our world: who I've talked to; what's going on with them; if I've scheduled him to speak someplace; and what that is going to look like, especially if it's a conference or an event with a lot of marketing potential. I take letters over the phone, go over flight schedules, and run all sorts of things by him.

"I use the phone to set up presentations and training programs, to answer questions, disseminate leads to our marketers, and field requests for materials and supplies. I have to be in a support role, in the middle between our outside contacts and Gordy, when he's on the road. So, I find out what they need to know and get back to them. I try not to leave people hanging with a question."

Let's say you take that advice seriously. When you reach your party you do all of the above—identify yourself and your company, state your purpose, and get quickly to the point. Have you licked the problem of wasted phone time? Well, you've certainly made a good beginning, but there is much more you can do to control your time.

It may surprise you to learn that most wasted phone time occurs when you are not even on the phone. The biggest time drain is incomplete or no preparation for the call. You get around that by putting together *callback preparation packets*, in which you include recent phone messages, correspondence, your call plan, and a blank sheet or form on which to take notes.

Am I kidding? No, I am not. Why would you carefully prepare for a face-to-face meeting but not for a phone meeting? Do you even know what your objective is, or is that some amorphous idea floating around in your mind? One of the best investments of your time you can make is to design a *call plan*.

This form will help you organize your calls before you make them, bring order to your thoughts, and focus on the reason for each call. The most important single item on the call plan is the specific objective you hope to accomplish during the call. This may be one objective or more than one. It may be fairly loose or tightly defined. But, whatever you do, know what you hope to achieve before you hang up; and, if you can't get that, what you will settle for. In addition, this form should include:

- ▸ The name of the caller (you or your boss)
- ▸ The person being called
- ▸ That person's company, phone number, and time zone
- ▸ The estimated time you will need to complete the call
- ▸ A couple of lines each for primary and secondary objectives
- ▸ The bare minimum you will accept
- ▸ Key questions you plan to ask
- ▸ Follow-up actions you will take after the call has been completed

You Gotta Have a System

Let's switch perspectives here. Up till now we've been focusing on part one of the equation—what *you* can do to improve your telephone effectiveness when *you* are the caller. Now, let's explore the other side of the coin—your role as the *receiver* of calls. As an administrative assistant, you are in a pivotal position to make your manager's life much easier if you fully understand this aspect of your job and are able to develop an effective *call-management system*. One of your most important job functions is to make it possible for your boss to accomplish more by eliminating interruptions and time-consuming activities that have a low return on investment of time and energy. You are, in every respect, an important partner in this effort.

Kathy Toennies receives about 20–25 calls a day. In her capacity as production manager for her company, she has those calls put through immediately. But when she switches hats and intercepts the company president's calls, she has to take a different approach.

"I don't have my calls screened because every call I get is pretty important. Most of them are calls I place first, and people are calling me back with questions or information on the jobs we're doing. Sometimes, however, I will take calls for my boss. If he can't come to the phone at that time, I do find it hard to go back to the person and say, 'He's in a meeting,' or 'He's not available.' I don't screen for anyone else in the company."

One of the first facets of any call-management system is whether or not, and in what manner, to screen calls. Callers, of course, don't like being screened. So, many secretaries just don't do it. On the other hand, screening has some very strong benefits, if it's done in a win-win style. If you do a good job of screening, you can help callers get answers to their questions faster by directing them to those who can really help them. You can save your boss the time and aggravation of needing to get out of calls with people he or she has no need or desire to talk to. You can be sure that both you and your boss will be focused on important calls, with background material in hand, allowing either of you, as well as the caller, to get more done in less time.

Cindy Eastwood is an administrative assistant in a three-person office. She spends most of her phone time talking to people seeking
jobs or companies seeking the perfect job applicant. Before she puts
any caller through, she has to glean some critical information.

"When candidates or clients call in, the first thing I want to
know is their name and the company they work for. Our account
executives speak with a large number of people in every day. While
a name alone may not 'ring a bell,' they usually recall the company
name. Some callers will not give out any information. They say, 'This
is John,' and that's all, or 'I'm returning his call. He'll know what I'm
calling about.' I try, tactfully, to explain that this is information I've
been asked to obtain."

Let's break callers down into three categories: people your boss
wants to talk to; people he or she doesn't want to talk to; and
people in the "uncertain" category. If your manager had more
information, he or she would be in a better position to decide.
The question is how do you know which is which? And the
answer is by asking the right kinds of questions and blending
curiosity with courtesy. This way, important callers don't get
caught up in phone tag, and neither you nor your boss wastes
valuable time on valueless calls. Your questions should address
all three of the possibilities we just mentioned. Let's say you
know the caller is someone your boss considers *important* and
wants to talk to.

> "Hello, Mr. Green. I'm glad you called. Barbara
> does want to talk with you and asked me to be alert for
> your call. I'd like to schedule a callback at a time when
> I know she'll be in her office. Is 2:30 this afternoon a
> good time for you, or would tomorrow morning be
> better?"

The tough ones, of course, are those callers you know your boss
doesn't want to talk to. These are a real test of skill and diplomacy.

"Ms. Carter, I can appreciate how much you believe in your printing company and want to talk with Mr. Howard. But we are very happy with our present printer and have no interest in changing at the present time. Mr. Howard has specifically asked me not to interrupt him with sales calls."

When you have insufficient information and just don't know, what do you do? Try this:

"Mr. Roberts, Ms. Connolly isn't available for phone calls right now, but I do work with her on arranging callback schedules. If you could tell me a little about your reason for calling, I'll do my best to help."

Mary Duda, CPS, is the right-hand person of a company president and CEO. As such, she does see her role as one of protector. What she protects, however, is her boss's *time*.

"I try to disseminate information in a fashion that will save his time. When an individual calls and wants to speak to Mr. M., I say, 'May I ask your name, and may I ask the nature of your call?' I gather all of the pertinent information. Often, Mr. M. is not the person they need to speak to. My job, I feel, is to get the caller to the place in our company that can be of the quickest service to them. For instance, Mr. M. would have no reason to talk to a machine salesperson because he does not purchase machinery. We have a whole department that does that. Therefore, I have to have an understanding of what our company does and who is involved in certain aspects of the business."

May I Take a Message, Please?

Messages matter, certainly within the context of any discussion of communication skills. You have to be a creative genius to write anything meaningful on those little pink *While You Were*

Out pads, so we suggest you design your own and include the following basics:

- ▸ *Name*, with phonetic spelling, if the correct pronunciation is not readily apparent
- ▸ *Company* and a description of the business, if your boss isn't familiar with it
- ▸ *Phone number*, location of area code, and time zone so you can schedule callbacks
- ▸ *Exact time, day, and date* the call came in
- ▸ *Reason* for the call

When Linda Yaniszewski's operators answer the phone for a client, to the caller, they *are* that client. The image they present is the image the caller forms of the client's company.

"Because we do service many small business people, as well as our larger clients, we do just about everything in the secretarial field—from resume writing to telephone answering. People who use our service have decided that they want a live person to answer their phone, in spite of the fact that they could utilize voice mail for a fraction of what it costs to use our service. That customer interaction is very important to their business. If it's bad, it can be devastating. For small businesses especially, we truly are their image—their clients' first impression of their company. That's why we work so hard on training our telephone operators to be considerate and to portray a professional image by the way they answer the phone."

Of course, this basic information is just what you would find on the little pink pads, so why design your own? Because there is other essential information that could and, indeed, should be included:

- ▸ *Emotions*, for one. How did the caller seem? Friendly? Testy? Professional? Polite? Note that.
- ▸ *Promises*, for another. If you tell the caller some action will be taken or that your boss will do something, but you fail to

mention this to your boss, it may be a promise broken. If it's in writing, everyone will have a record, and you can follow up.

▶ *Last contact* is important, too. When you can, attach copies of recent phone messages or written correspondence so your boss has something to refer to.

▶ *Impressions* are the last thing to add to your custom-designed form. Listen between the lines to nonverbal cues. Use your intuition. And jot down your impressions. The caller communicates things only *you* will hear and your boss, who never spoke directly to this person, will not. Your impressions, therefore, are very important.

When the phone rings, chances are you weren't just sitting there waiting for it to ring. You were busy, and the call most likely interrupted your train of thought. If you have a phone center, at least you can focus your mind on the call and turn away from visual distractions. Though you have already read an entire chapter on listening, *phone listening* skills bear mentioning here.

➡

Katie Olney's phone rings constantly, and she never knows who is going to be on the other end of the line. Sometimes it's someone returning her call, sometimes a facilitator of her company's training programs, sometimes an interested person who has heard her boss speak. She fields calls from company presidents, printers, and parole officers—all with the same unfailing cheerful tone and ready laugh.

"I think I'm strong on the telephone. I'm very comfortable with it. I can talk for a long time, and I am able to build relationships with people I've never met. I deal with people all over the country, sometimes for years, before I meet them. I see the telephone as an asset instead of looking at it with trepidation. Our phones are always busy, sometimes with more calls than I can handle. I simply deal with whatever crisis I have to handle at the moment and trust that people will be understanding if I have to call them back. I am very good about getting back to them as fast as I can, and I do try to bring some humor to most situations."

➡

Seeking to Understand

If you want to be sure you really hear what is being said, and what is *not* being said, while keeping you and the other person on track, here are eight simple guidelines:

1. *Prepare to listen.* That means purposely clearing your mind of what you were thinking about, and focusing it on listening.

2. *Turn away from your other work.* That means both physically and psychologically. Forget it for the moment. If you have a phone center, that will be easier to do because everything you need will be right there in front of you.

3. *Keep an open mind.* Try to understand what the other person is saying, and give them time to say it all.

4. *Let the other person speak without interruption.* If he or she wanders, bring the conversation back on track with a well-placed question.

5. *Provide feedback.* Let the caller know you hear and understand what is being said.

6. *Sit as you would if that person were opposite your desk.* Look in the mirror, and be sure your voice reflects a face that projects friendliness.

7. *Take notes during the call,* preferably on a form you have created just for that purpose. Get the facts, but also record your impressions and reactions.

8. *Repeat and verify all key facts.* It's important to get that information down correctly, especially names, dates, and time. Read it back. If you're wrong, you want to know before the end of the call, not when it's too late.

There are only two account executives in Cindy Eastwood's office, but between them they field a lot of phone calls in a single day. As the person who answers the phone, Cindy is the nerve center of the office.

"Our account executives work with many foreign-born people

in the biotech and pharmaceutical industries. I have a problem pronouncing the names, so I ask for the spelling and let the account executive figure out how to pronounce them. Fortunately, they are very good at that. I always try to repeat what the caller says, especially phone numbers. If the account executive isn't available, I will ask, 'Do you want to leave a message, or would you prefer to call back?'

"My system for taking messages is to make notes on a separate piece of paper, edit, and then write the message on a message pad with carbon duplicates, so I have a record of all calls. I transfer only the pertinent data. How do I know what's pertinent? That comes with knowing your candidate and your account executives."

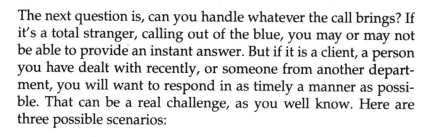

The next question is, can you handle whatever the call brings? If it's a total stranger, calling out of the blue, you may or may not be able to provide an instant answer. But if it is a client, a person you have dealt with recently, or someone from another department, you will want to respond in as timely a manner as possible. That can be a real challenge, as you well know. Here are three possible scenarios:

▸ "Marketing Department . . . this is Jean. How can I help you? [*pause*] Yes, Mr. Arnold, of course I remember that conversation. [*pause*] No, I don't; but if you'll hold on a moment, I'll see if I can locate that information." Jean puts Mr. Arnold on hold and frantically searches for the right file. Worst case, she can't find what she is looking for and says, "I am so sorry, Mr. Arnold, but that file doesn't seem to be handy. Would it be possible for me to get back to you in a few minutes?"

▸ Better, but still not perfect, would be this kind of response, after some drawer opening and paper shuffling: "Thank you for holding, Mr. Arnold. I apologize for keeping you waiting, but I have that information in front of me now."

▸ Even better—best case, in fact—would be if Jean could immediately respond: "Yes, of course, Mr. Arnold. I have that file right here on my desk. Let me just turn to the sheet you want to discuss, and I'll be happy to answer your question."

Impossible? Not at all, if you are prepared with the information you will probably need, and that information is close at hand.

———————————————————————▶

Beth Quick-Andrews views almost every aspect of her business—especially her phone—as a "sales tool." She uses it to her greatest advantage by never leaving things to chance. Even her answering machine message, though upbeat and brief, is a subtle sales pitch for Quick Business Services.

"The telephone is a sales tool. It's another form of communication with whomever is on the other end of the phone—whether that's a client, a vendor, or a relative. Returning phone calls promptly is a sales tool. Leaving clear messages, so I'm not wasting the other person's time and I'm giving them as much information as possible, is a sales tool. Speaking clearly and sounding cheerful are sales tools. These are all opportunities for that person to get an impression of me and what I'm about."

———————————————————————▶

Summing Up

I think you can clearly see just how critical telephone skills are to the communication part of your job. In this chapter, you have seen the value of having your own private phone center and what it takes to set one up; seven ways you can put an end to phone tag; all the things voice mail can do for you; effective strategies for getting around inefficient phone systems and bureaucracies; and a host of ways to improve your efficiency whether you initiate the call or someone calls you.

No matter how much state-of-the-art equipment you have crammed into your work space to help you communicate, you may be surprised to learn that your most expressive communication device is your own body. In Chapter 6, we turn our attention to communicating without words. What is known as *nonverbal communication* is sometimes more eloquent and often more honest than all the lovely words we can say or write.

Chapter 6

Speaking Without Words

If you've ever been told that you are as easy to read as an open book or that your facial expression gives you away, you have some idea of how much you communicate without even speaking. Communication that requires no words—spoken or written—yet has a language all its own is called *nonverbal*. You use it all the time. In fact, it is one of your primary vehicles of transmitting messages. Obviously, no discussion of communication skills, particularly in the business world, would be complete without it.

Every minute you spend interacting with someone else you are sending messages of some kind. Nonverbal communication is made up of all the ways in which you send those messages. You don't have to say a word to communicate volumes of information, often without even being aware of it. Obviously, we feel that it's far better for your message sending to be a conscious act than an unconscious one.

Carol Green is a perfectionist. She admits to being too critical of herself and others when it comes to projecting the right professional image. To her, little things do mean a lot.

"When I was in the Marketing Department, everything had to be perfect. My boss used to say, 'Whatever comes out of Marketing—whether it is internal or external—it is telling the company and the world that this is the way we do things.' If we are casual-looking or if our office is a mess, people immediately assume that everybody in the company operates that way. Marketing is the front line, and if

Marketing puts out something that is wrong or something that is sloppy, that is how the world forms its impression of our company."

That is the purpose of this chapter—to increase your awareness and understanding of the nonverbal messages you send and receive. By the time you finish reading it, you will understand how important the first ten seconds of any encounter can be; the eloquence of body language; the roles your eyes, face, and posture play in communicating; and how to interpret other people's gestures and use your own to send the messages you want to send. Along the way, you will also be introduced to a few little gems, including: gesture clusters, walking and talking styles, what you can learn from a handshake, the dance of the hands, body rhythms, and the importance of space.

Kathy Toennies could wear jeans to work if she wanted to, but she doesn't want to. Even in a small company where she has little client contact, she is conscious of how she looks and dresses. To Kathy, what she wears has a profound effect not only on how she thinks other people see her but on how she sees herself.

"I think the way somebody looks and dresses is very important in terms of a first impression. If I'm dressed in a suit or a nice dress, I feel that I look better. I also think people take women more seriously when we dress up. I don't see people on a regular basis. If I know I'll be seeing clients, I will dress up; but even if nobody is coming in, I'll still wear something nice. In my last job, I wore a dress or a suit four days out of five. It was a much bigger company, and I think that makes a difference. Also, there were sales reps all over the place, and they wore jackets every day. Here, there are not that many people, but all of the men who work here do wear shirts and ties."

If all this sounds like a long way from what you thought you needed to know to be a secretary, you may change your mind.

In fact, this may be the single most important set of skills in your growing repertoire.

The Instant Inventory

Let's start at the beginning, which is usually the first time a stranger looks at you. What does that person see, and how important is it? The answers are *more than you realize* and *very important*. Here's why. First impressions are lasting impressions, and it takes only ten seconds to form them. What can someone see in ten seconds? Well, starting at the top and swooping down to your feet in an S-shaped visual inventory, the very first thing an observer would see is your *form*—including your size and shape—which will either attract or turn off that person's attention. Your form says a great deal about you, even if it's totally inaccurate.

→

Becky Jordan knows all about the ten-second once-over. In fact, she uses it to make her own instant assessments.

"I look at people's eyes first, and then I look at their shoes. People who don't make eye contact drive me crazy. Wimpy handshakes do, too. One of my pet peeves is someone who cups his hand so you don't touch his palm when you shake his hand. I find that very telling."

→

Tall people are viewed as leaders. Overweight people are often thought to be lazy or slow. If you're taller than the other person, you may intimidate. If you're shorter, you may be overlooked. If you think of your own form as pretty much a given, it's good to know that even if you can't change its fundamental structure you *can* change other people's perception of how it appears to them. One simple way is to take a deep breath, stand up straight, pull in your stomach, and set your shoulders back. With this relatively modest adjustment to your posture, you can instantly convey a sense of energy, influence, and power—no matter what your body shape or height.

———————————————————————————▶

Though Beth Quick-Andrews is in the secretarial services business, she has never viewed herself as a secretary. Instead, her self-image is one of a business owner who provides a valuable resource to other people. Nonverbally, she conveys that perception to potential clients in her bearing and in the places in which she meets them.

"Since I own my own company, I have a vested interest in the work I do for my clients. I think one thing that helps me is *where* I meet my clients. Within professional associations, because we serve on committees together, they treat me as a colleague or peer. They tend to perceive me more as an equal than as an employee. The fact that I'm young and a woman can be a stumbling block. Often, men have a tough time dealing with me; though, overall, I find I have had fewer problems being accepted by male clients than by female ones in terms of valuing the services I offer."

———————————————————————————▶

What does the observer see next? Your *face* or, as image consultants like to call it, your *communication center*. Your face, particularly your eyes, communicates your personality. So, if you don't make eye contact, your personality remains a mystery. Your face, by the way, must be seen. If you wear dark glasses or have hair covering most of it, you may give the impression that you're hiding something.

The sweeping S-shape viewing ends at your *feet*. If your face is your personality, and your form is your power base, your feet are your character. One supposedly can judge a person by something as simple as shoes and socks. Scuffed, unpolished, or unrepaired shoes and saggy, baggy, torn socks or hose are considered character defects. Supposedly, they demonstrate a lack of concern for detail and an inability to follow through.

———————————————————————————▶

If you don't want to worry about that ten seconds, Patricia Diana of Bridge Information Systems suggests you plan ahead and deal with the impression you make *before* 9:00 A.M. That's especially true if your company has a designated casual day.

"You send off some really important signals with your clothing and your hair and your general appearance. Those are things you can be sensitive to *before* you ever get into the office. I wear business suits and blouses and skirts. I generally do not wear pants unless its casual day. Casual day is a nice time to express yourself, but you still have to be professional. You may dress casually and feel casual, but it's tricky because you shouldn't totally let your hair down. You're still being paid to do your job. You're still expected to be neatly dressed and well groomed. My boss usually wears a lightweight summer suit, and I wear a nice pants suit. My casual is more *business casual.*"

That's it. Ten seconds and you've been sized up from hair follicles to toenails and found acceptable or dismissable. And this is before you have said one single word! This initial and possibly indelible impression is made from information gathered by simply looking at you. There is probably no more dramatic demonstration of nonverbal communication than this. Yet, it is really little more than an introduction to the topic.

You also communicate nonverbally through a number of other observable externals, all of which convey distinct messages to an astute observer. What you're wearing, how you are groomed, your choice of accessories, and dozens of similar details are all clues to who you are and what you stand for. You probably recognize that all of these elements fall under the general heading of professional image, a subject with which you are already familiar.

Sue St. John learned how misleading first impressions can be in one of her very first jobs. As someone who administrated psychological and assessment tests to potential job candidates, she had countless opportunities to check out the validity of such instant judgments.

"I remember waiting to test a man and expecting a very unappealing person to walk in the door. Why? Because all I knew about this person was his name, which was *Billy Bobo*. You can imagine the picture I conjured up in my mind. Well, in walked a man with all this energy . . . intelligence in his eyes . . . and a marvelous, firm handshake. His first words were, 'Hi! Nice to meet you. I'm Bill Bobo!' He looked right into my soul. His total presence obliterated everything I had expected to see. I was so impressed by meeting him that suddenly his name did not seem one bit funny to me. In a split second, he went from being *Silly Billy Bobo* to the perfect person for the job. He was, of course, hired by the prestigious brokerage firm that had ordered the testing.

"I tested a lot of people over an eight-year period, and I used to play a game with myself—trying to guess how well each one would do in the testing. I could tell a great deal about them by the expressions on their faces, how straight they sat up in a chair, whether they had a sense of humor about being locked up in a little room for five hours. More often than not, my first impression mirrored the results of our sophisticated personality tests—so often, in fact, that I was surprised when they didn't."

The Body Speaks

To really get a handle on nonverbal communication, you must go beyond these basic elements of your external packaging and move into the area of *body language*. Every single part of your body communicates in its own way. Everything you do, every gesture, every nuance, every motion —no matter how tiny—says something. Whether or not you look someone in the eye when you speak . . . your handshake . . . how much or how little you respect people's *personal space* . . . your posture . . . your mannerisms . . . the energy you exude . . . your sincerity or lack of it . . . your unspoken confidence level . . . and your annoying habits —all send messages.

Since others take your measure in a ten-second inventory that starts at the top and sweeps down to your feet, we will describe nonverbal communication in the same way, beginning with the most compelling and revealing feature—*the eyes*.

The Mirrors of the Soul

When you look at another person, you both know something about your relationship, no matter how brief that relationship may turn out to be. You may know that you are pleased to be together or that you are angry or that you are sexually attracted to each other. You can read another person's face without meeting his or her eyes; but when eyes do meet, not only do you know how the other person feels, but that person knows you know. Nothing is hidden in that glance, which is why eye contact makes all of us feel open and exposed and vulnerable.

➤

A big part of Kathy Toennies's job as production manager for Ideas to Images involves interaction with other people. Yet, despite her public speaking and communications training with Dale Carnegie, she admits that she still has a little trouble *locking eyes.*

"I do have problems with eye contact. I tend to keep looking away, especially when I'm speaking. It's easier for me to look at someone when they are talking to me than when I'm talking to them."

➤

Most encounters begin with eye contact. Yet, eye behavior is perhaps the subtlest form of body language. Culture programs us in childhood, teaching us what to do with our eyes and what to expect other people to do with theirs. As a result, when you shift your eyes and meet another person's gaze, or fail to meet it, you produce an effect that is many times more powerful than the small movement of your eye muscles that preceded it.

Eye movements can convey attitudes and feelings, as well as reveal personalities. For example, if you are embarrassed or upset, you will usually try to avoid meeting the eyes of others. You are likely to do less looking when asked highly personal questions than when you are asked neutral ones. And if you tell a lie, you may be perceived as becoming *shifty-eyed.*

Women and men have somewhat different eye behavior— something worth taking note of in your profession. Women do more looking than men do, and once they have made eye contact, they tend to hold it longer. Among men, and other animals, looking patterns often reflect status. When a top monkey catches the eye of a lesser monkey, for example, the one of lower status will usually narrow its eyes or look away. Whenever two monkeys lock eyes and one looks away, both know who is in control. Next time you're in a meeting, you might conduct a little informal study of who is looking at whom and who is looking away. It really does speak volumes.

⟶

Even though she has only been working in the state legislature for a relatively short time, Kathy Pierce has mastered the art of communication in a variety of ways. Sometimes, she has learned, the less said, the better.

"Gestures, first impressions, body language . . . all those things . . . are very important in this job. Often, you want to get a certain representative's attention, but you don't want to interrupt her. If there are a couple of representatives and a couple of senators talking, and you have a call you know one of them is going to want to take, just being able to make eye contact is enough to let her know. That way, you are not interrupting all the time. Yet, you can maintain communication without speaking.

"Towards the end of the session, these legislators are on the floor, sometimes until midnight or two o'clock in the morning. Then, they go home and are back in session at 9:00 the next morning. You can tell how it's going on the floor by the way they come *off* the floor. Their facial expressions and body language, their clenched fists, their quietness, or just the way they walk all let you know whether they're just taking a break or if they get to go home."

⟶

Your Communications Center

When you tear your gaze away from someone's eyes, you begin to see the rest of that person's *face*. In fact, we all focus on the face more often than on any other part of the body, and facial expressions have widely accepted meanings. You have no doubt experienced a look that could kill, a come-hither look, or the steely glance. And you have probably concluded that when people don't look at you when they speak or when you speak to them, they're trying to hide something.

If the eyes are the mirrors of the soul, the face is the television screen for everything else. A British research team isolated and catalogued 135 distinct gestures and expressions of face, head, and body, of which eighty were strictly face and head gestures. They recorded nine separate smiles, each with a different message. Smiles, however, should not always be associated with happy faces.

Sharyn Lenz does try to focus on the other people's eyes when she's involved in a conversation; but in a noisy high school, sometimes she finds that isn't really the most effective way to understand what's being said.

"When I look at somebody, and there's a lot of noise around us, I can't look at their eyes. If I don't look at their mouth, I can't concentrate on what they're saying. That bothers me because I do think eye contact is very important, and I'm sure they can tell that I'm looking at their mouth. Also, when someone cannot look me in the face, I feel I'm not getting the whole story."

Facial expressions can also express shock or great surprise, conflict or anger, disbelief, admiration, skepticism, hurt feelings, and a host of other emotions. In a series of articles on nonverbal communications for the *T&D Journal*, author George Porter noted that displeasure or confusion are revealed by a frown, envy or disbelief by a raised eyebrow, and defensiveness by simply tightening the lips.

While most bosses aren't actually mind readers, they do seem to be very good at reading between the lines of what you don't say. Patricia Diana thinks unconscious facial expressions and other nonverbal signals may be sending messages you'd rather not send.

"My boss tends to be very perceptive. He can kind of sense if I don't want to do something he's asked me to do. You have to be very sensitive to your response when your boss asks you to do something. You don't want to hesitate. What he or she is asking of you is most likely within reason. You're being paid to do it, and you should really be there and available to say "yes" without hesitancy. I don't think you should doubt or challenge him (or her) unless he asks for your advice or unless you think he's really headed in the wrong direction. You have to use your judgment on that. But most of the time, just say, 'Sure I would be happy to do that.' "

➡

Speaking in Code

While the face is endlessly fluid and fascinating, it is not the only part of our bodies that communicates. Anthropologist Edward Sapir noted: "We respond to *gestures* with an extreme alertness and, one might almost say, in accordance with an elaborate code that is written nowhere, known by none, and understood by all."

What part do gestures play in communication? And how can they possibly compete with the rich and subtle nuances of the human voice and the wonders of language? They are, in fact, critically important and enriching in their own right. Gestures convey everything from your tension level to your personal style. They do all of this on a hidden level, beneath your awareness. But whether you are aware or not, this communication registers; and you do respond to it.

Sigmund Freud observed that "the unconscious of one human being can react upon that of another without passing through the conscious." These unconscious reactions then become untested facts to which we respond. If we subconsciously interpret a gesture as unfriendly, we consciously react to it in an equally unfriendly manner.

At first, it's difficult to view gestures objectively; but with awareness and practice it becomes much easier, just like learning any language. With very few exceptions, people nonverbally communicate their inner feelings quite openly. If what they *say* is consistent with what they *reveal* through their gestures, they are probably telling the truth. How do you know? One way is to look for consistency between verbal and nonverbal communications. If the words are friendly, but you sense hostility, the words may be deceiving.

Mary Hammond, a partner in Executive Assistance in Phoenix, Arizona, has mastered the art of reading body language. Literally on the front lines, she is the first one people see when they walk into her office. Her challenge, as she sees it, is twofold: (1) to make each person feel welcome, and (2) to assess that person's mood, style, and expectations—very quickly.

"When people walk in—especially the tenants I deal with all the time—I know immediately if I'm going to have a hard day with them or if it's going to be a day when we'll all get along. I can tell just by the way they walk in. If they're rushing, I know to be on the alert. I sense that I will have to be more professional, more service oriented than usual. I do read from their body language where they are and unconsciously adjust my own response and behavior. One person may be in a very tense, tight mood; another will come bounding in with not a care in the world. So, I find myself bouncing back and forth within a matter of minutes just to be appropriate to each person's mood."

Let's look at a few familiar gestures and see how obvious their meanings become when we think about them. *Open hands* are often associated with sincerity and openness. So is an *unbuttoned coat or jacket.* Have you ever noticed, for example, how men who are open or friendly toward you will frequently unbutton their coats or even take them off in your presence? And, if open hands and unbuttoned coats signal openness, *closed, folded arms* and *buttoned-up coats* indicate the opposite.

In a meeting, it might help to know that someone who has

just favorably changed his mind might unconsciously signal that piece of information by instinctively uncrossing his arms and unbuttoning his coat. When negotiations are going well, seated individuals tend to unbutton their coats, uncross their legs, and move up toward the edge of their chairs or closer to the conference table.

If there is any gesture you can usually spot, it's the crossed-arm position. Crossed arms appear to act as a protective shield against an anticipated attack or a way of maintaining a fixed position. Since women have an upper torso structure that differs from men's, they fold their arms considerably lower on the body. This gesture—in both men and women—is one of the easiest to understand, yet the least recognized nonverbal indicator.

If you're wondering whether a co-worker is defensive or just standing in a comfortable position, notice his or her hands. Do they seem relaxed, or are the fingers wrapped around the biceps in a strangle hold that is turning the person's knuckles white? White knuckles are a sure sign of tension.

Dancing Hands

Few parts of the body are as expressive as the *hands*, which often seem to be engaged in a dance of their own. We all know people who would surely be rendered speechless if you tied up their hands. But it's also true that most of us would actually be pretty uncomfortable if we were forced to talk without the little gestures that accompany and illustrate our words. You are quite aware of what others are doing with their hands; but in general you may ignore it, assuming that it's just so much meaningless motion. But is it really meaningless? Probably not.

Gestures do communicate. Sometimes they help clarify, when the verbal message is unclear. At other times, they can unintentionally reveal emotions. Tightly clasped hands or hands that fidget are clues to tension that other people are apt to pick up. Sometimes, too, a gesture is so clearly functional that the exact meaning is unmistakable—like pointing a finger in a certain direction or beckoning for someone to come closer. Some of the most common gestures are actually tied to speech as ways to illustrate or emphasize what is said.

When you, yourself, are gesturing, you're probably only peripherally aware of doing it. And while you might be slightly more aware of others' gestures, in general, you would be more apt to look at their faces than at their hands. Yet, the hands are marvelously articulate. Seven hundred thousand different hand signals are possible using various combinations of postures and arm, wrist, and finger movements. Throughout history, there have been sign languages in which gestures actually replaced speech. In fact, man's earliest language may have been made up completely of gestures.

Revealing Posture

Posture is the easiest of the nonverbal clues to pick up. The first thing to watch for is the *postural echo.* People literally echo or mimic one another's body attitudes. Have you ever noticed how two people who have worked together for a long time will sit in precisely the same way? Or perhaps they *mirror-image* each other—crossing the opposite leg, moving the opposite arm—like a direct reflection.

Like so many people, Sharyn Lenz insists she can't talk without her hands. Since that is her way of expressing herself, she pays close attention to other people's hands and to all the aspects of their body language.

"I think I can tell how people are going to respond at a parent conference by the way they're sitting in the chair. If they're sitting sideways with their shoulder to me, I know right away that I'm going to have to break through before they will share anything with me. I also know that if I'm sitting in a chair in a relaxed position, people automatically think I have nothing to do. What I have learned to do is keep talking but stand up and move toward a different spot. That seems to let people know that I'm on my way to my next task. Kids can really talk for a long time, and I never want to hurt anyone's feelings."

Whenever people share a point of view they often seem to share a posture as well. Just as congruent postures express rapport, incongruent postures can be used to establish psychological distance. Shifts in posture appear to parallel spoken language just as gestures sometimes do. During conversations people may shift their heads and eyes every few sentences, just as they have finished making a point. Or, they may shift their bodies completely to coincide with a change in point of view.

Like everyone else, you have a characteristic way of holding your body when you sit, stand, and walk. It's as personal as your signature, and many think it offers a reliable clue to your character. Most of us can recognize people we know well even when they are still a long distance away by the way they walk or even stand. For many social situations in our culture, there are postures that are considered proper and improper. For instance, one doesn't lie down during a business meeting or prop one's feet on the table at dinner. You know that you can quite deliberately convey a message by assuming a posture that is inappropriate to the situation.

Posture is not only a clue to character; it's also an expression of attitude—revealing much about your feelings toward the people you are with at the moment. Among Americans, posture can be a tip-off not only to relative status but to whether people like one another or not. Those who are outside the action, standing on the periphery of a group, in small ways hold their bodies differently than insiders do. Typically, they stand with their weight on just one foot rather than on both, perhaps with their hands propped on their hips and their heads up. Someone who is really involved in the group, on the other hand, will lean forward a little and tip his or her head forward.

A researcher who has studied posture on a global scale catalogued roughly 1,000 static postures that are both anatomically possible and relatively comfortable. From those 1,000, each culture selects its own quite limited repertoire. We, in the West, tend to forget that there are other ways to sit and stand besides the ones we're accustomed to. Every culture has postures it considers proper and others held to be improper, though what is polite in one society could be just short of scandalous in the next. If your organization is multinational in its business dealings, it's worth doing some investigation on the cultural norms of those with whom you work.

Feel the Beat

Professor Eliot Condon is a *kinesicist*—someone who studies the relationship between nonlinguistic body motions and communication. He is particularly interested in *body rhythms*. "In minute ways," says Condon, "a person's body dances continually to the beat of his own speech." When you talk, your hand and finger movements, head nods, eye blinks—all the motions you make—fall in with the beat. The listener also moves in time with the speech of the speaker.

This is called *interactional synchrony.* It's subtle—not an exact mirroring of gestures—but simply a shared beat. It usually happens too quickly and too subtly to catch with the naked eye. What purpose could it possibly serve if we're not even conscious of it? Condon believes it is the bedrock on which human communication is built. Without it, in his opinion, communication might not be possible at all.

Rhythm plays other roles in human communication. People are enormously regular in their patterns of listening and speaking. Apparently, your conversational rhythm is one of your most stable and predictable characteristics and reveals quite a lot about how you relate to other people. Everyone uses conversational rhythms to interpret relationships. If you stop and think about it, you can characterize almost anybody you know by describing his or her speech pattern. One person responds only after a thoughtful pause and speaks slowly with lengthy pauses. Another leaps in to finish your thought for you, takes off on a tangent of his or her own, and abruptly stops talking.

Words are distracting. We're too preoccupied with *what* other people are saying to take notice of *how* they are saying it. Yet, if you could negate the words and substitute nonsense syllables, the meaning of *when* and *how long* people talk would become much clearer.

How much you talk and your pattern of speech determine the way people react to you. If you do most of the talking, you are apt to be chosen as leader. If you frequently interrupt, people may assume you're out to dominate. If you leap in eagerly when there is a break in the conversation, you will probably be regarded as a go-getter or self-starter. From earliest childhood, your basic rhythms affect your relations with others, and it's a good bet they continue to do so in your professional life.

Rhythm also reveals itself in the way you walk. Like everyone else, you have a distinctive walk that makes you easily recognizable. Certain characteristics are due in part to your body structure; but pace, length of stride, and posture seem to change with your emotions. Haven't you ever noticed that when people are dejected, they shuffle along with their hands in their pockets, seldom looking up or noticing where they are headed? Or the guy who walks with his hands on his hips? That person is more like a sprinter than a long-distance runner. He seems to want to go the shortest possible distance in the fastest possible time to reach his goal.

Can't you always tell when your boss is preoccupied with a problem by the way he or she walks—head down, hands clasped behind the back? On the other hand, a raised chin, arms exaggerated in their swing, and deliberate and firm pace all signal that things are going very well.

Extending a Hand

Let's revisit the hands for just a moment. Men are taught—from childhood on—how to "shake hands like a man," how to grip the other person's hand, how to squeeze it firmly, and how to release it. But no one, it seems, teaches a little girl how to shake hands like a woman. Women tend to develop firm handshakes out of self-defense, because they encounter businessmen who automatically extend their hand in greeting. Unfortunately, many men don't seem to know what to do with a woman's hand once they have it. In almost universal disfavor is the clammy handshake, but it's not the only culprit. A man who extends his hand to a woman may produce a handshake that ranges from a dead fish to a bone crusher. This is another reason so many women in business have learned to take the lead and control the amount of pressure in the handshake, no matter who initiates it.

Handshaking customs vary from country to country. The French shake hands on entering and leaving a room. The Germans pump hands one time and one time only. Some Africans snap their fingers after each handshake. Still others consider handshaking in bad taste. Whatever the situation, find out the local custom before making the assumption that your brand of handshake will be acceptable.

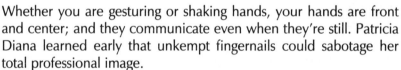

Whether you are gesturing or shaking hands, your hands are front and center; and they communicate even when they're still. Patricia Diana learned early that unkempt fingernails could sabotage her total professional image.

"How you put yourself together matters. Manicures are very important in New York. I literally have been told, 'Do not go out on a job interview if your nail polish is chipped.' Maybe it is different in New York, Boston, or Chicago, where more is expected of you. But wherever you are, people like to see someone who is well groomed and well put together. It really is a plus. If people don't know you, all they have to go on is the outer shell. When I meet people, sometimes I don't get to say much more than, 'Hi, how are you?' and 'Come on into the office. Rick is ready to see you.' All that they see are my clothes and my hair and how well put together I am. I want to make a good impression for my boss's sake. He wants that, and he pays me for that."

The Invisible Bubble

An important aspect of nonverbal communication is one that seems to have little to do with our bodies. It is the *space around our bodies* that counts. Edward Hall, professor of anthropology at Northwestern University, explains that a person's sense of self isn't bounded by his skin. "We walk around inside a kind of private bubble that represents the amount of airspace we feel we must have between ourselves and other people," says Hall. You can easily demonstrate this by moving gradually in on another person. At some point, the other person will begin—irritably or just absentmindedly—to back away.

Misunderstandings can develop because people from different cultures handle space in very different ways. For two unacquainted North American adult males, the comfortable distance to stand for conversations is about two feet apart. The South American, on the other hand, prefers to stand much closer, which creates problems when a South American and a North American meet face-to-face. If Americans and Latins have misunderstandings about maintaining a sociable distance, Americans and Arabs are even less compatible in their space habits. Arabs belong to a touch culture and, in conversation, seem to thrive on close contact.

Elnor Hickman has learned about international communication and customs the hard way, through trying to get some information through to Brazil. Unfortunately, she discovered, she had to try *everything*—fax, phone calls, and written communication—to make sure that her message was getting through. But technology is only one small part of international communications.

"I think this is an area that is going to get a lot of attention as more and more businesses go global. Understanding the nuances of international communication is a whole new area and will require a willingness on the part of the individual to learn and to be able to do the right thing. At our international conference, I am going to learn a lot. My company is not global or national or even statewide. All of our services are limited to the city of Chicago. I'm really in for an awakening in this conference with people from around the world. I'm probably going to learn more than anyone else there."

Relatively speaking, Americans live in a nontouch-touch culture, partly due to our Puritan heritage. We spend years teaching our children not to crowd in or lean on us. In situations where you are forced to stand very close to another person—on a crowded subway or in an elevator—don't you tend to compensate by averting your eyes, turning away, and tensing your muscles if you are accidentally touched? Most people do.

The degree of closeness can convey a threat, but it can also convey messages far subtler than that. There is a whole scale of distances, each thought to be appropriate in this country for a particular kind of relationship. Contact up to 18 inches, for example, is treated as very personal distance. Two and a half to four feet, which still keeps most people at arm's length, is considered appropriate for discussing personal matters. In an office, people who work together normally stand four to seven feet apart to talk.

On the other hand, if your boss is a man, and he stands four to seven feet from where you are sitting and looks down at you, that tends to have a domineering effect. Choosing the right distance can be crucial for political, personal, and even physical reasons. Human beings seem to not only have strong feelings about space but a real biological need for enough elbow room in which to function.

Americans have other unspoken rules about space. When two or more people are talking together in public, they assume that the ground they're standing on is—temporarily at least—their own joint territory and that others won't intrude. And they are usually right.

People sometimes try to stake out a claim to a chunk of public territory just by the location they select, like taking a middle chair along the side of an empty table in a library. The relative position a person chooses can be a status signal. The senior executive in a gathering, as an example, will automatically gravitate to the end chair at a rectangular table. If co-workers stand in a circle, it's a safe bet that everyone is on a more or less equal footing.

Space communicates volumes when a number of people cluster together in a conversational knot, especially in an informal setting. Each individual defines positioning in the group by where he or she stands. By choosing a certain distance, you indicate how intimate you want to be; by choosing a location, such as the head spot, you can signal what kind of role you hope to play. When the group settles into a particular configuration and all the shifting around stops, it's a sign that nonverbal negotiations are over, at least for now.

━━━━━━━━━━━━━━━━━━━━━━━━━━━━━━━▶

If people make a statement by where they position themselves in a group, they also make one by where they choose *not* to sit or stand. Sharyn Lenz, for example, would never take the chair at the head of a conference table, because that would send an inaccurate message.

"We very seldom have meetings, but when we do I would not want anyone to think *I think* I'm in charge. If my boss is at the meeting, I will sit next to her. And if everyone is clustered at one end of the table, I would probably sit at the other end. If you sit with a certain group of people, others will automatically assume that you all think the same way. Sometimes that's just not the case at all."

━━━━━━━━━━━━━━━━━━━━━━━━━━━━━━━▶

The Rest of the Senses

What we say and how we move our bodies are only two of the more obvious forms of communication. We also communicate by touch, smell, and, on rare occasions, even taste. These senses can form an important part of the total message, yet we know very little about them. Americans underestimate the importance of the nose as a message receiver. In fact, we are so reluctant to smell one another that we actually suppress our sense of smell. We are an overdeodorized society, and it seems that every year advertisers discover new odors that must immediately be banished. We live in fear of bad breath, body odor, house odor, any kind of odor. There also seem to be determined attempts to replace natural odors with manufactured ones—perfumes, shaving lotions, etc.

Not only are we reluctant to smell one another, we don't go in for touching either. Yet, touch has a special kind of immediacy, for when one person touches another the experience is, by its very nature, mutual. Skin contacts skin, directly or through layers of clothing; and there is instant awareness on both sides. Touching—at least of an impersonal sort—goes on all around us whether we see it or not, but the very fact that we read it out of so many situations indicates something about our attitudes toward it. Touch, taste, and smell are the close-range senses. Hearing and seeing, on the other hand, can offer experience from a distance. All of them are vehicles through which we communicate with each other without speaking, listening, or reading. These are the carriers of our nonverbal messages.

Summing Up

While the whole concept of nonverbal communications is probably not new to you, you may not have realized how powerful a tool you have at your disposal. If you take a little time to closely observe others—perhaps conduct your own ten-second, S-shaped inventory; think about that first handshake; and take note of whether body language conflicts with words—you can master the art of reading the silent cues. But reading well is only half the equation; the other half is sending the messages you intend to send rather than the ones you unconsciously send. The more you understand nonverbal communication, the better able you are to communicate accurately and purposefully to others.

Chapter 7

Good-bye Cyberphobia

No one has to tell you that one of the most dramatic changes in your job in recent years has been the computerization of the workplace. Even if you are a relative newcomer to the secretarial field, the sophistication of the hardware and software you encounter on the job seems to escalate by the day. Imagine, then, that only a few years ago an IBM, self-correcting Selectric was considered state-of-the-art. Today, you'd be hard pressed to find it, or *any* typewriter, around in any great numbers. If typewriters are used at all, it is usually for such mundane tasks as dashing off a few labels or an envelope.

Virtually everyone has a personal computer on his or her desk, including your boss. Cyberphopia—fear of computers—is considered laughable, and computer illiteracy is totally unacceptable. But literacy means more than being able to function in a word processing program. Secretaries and administrative assistants are also expected to function with databases, spreadsheets, graphics programs, time and billing, networks, modems, client and time management programs, and more.

Quick Business Services is a computer-based administrative services company. Beth Quick-Andrews is equally conversant with IBM and Macintosh and lists the following software packages in the *Annual Membership Directory of the National Association of Secretarial Services (NASS)*: Quicken, MS Word, WordPerfect, MS Excel, Page-Maker, and database packages.

"With the way technology has overtaken the business world, to *not* be computer literate today is to be at an extreme disadvantage.

It's very rare that anyone uses a typewriter to do anything but type an envelope. Today's technology not only provides a much more efficient way of doing things but has also set an expectation for timeliness and accuracy. Work must be done quickly and sent quickly, by fax, modem, or e-mail. And the expectations of what can be done on the job have changed dramatically as well. Administrative assistants are doing things in-house that used to be sent to a typesetter, a service bureau, or even a printer.

"I offer my clients—which range from small businesses to independent salespeople to large corporations—graphic design, direct mail, and secretarial services on a project basis. Actually, I do anything an administrative assistant in an office would do. I manage databases, do mail-merge letters, put labels on envelopes, lay out brochures and newsletters, transcribe tapes, prepare invoices, type correspondence and contracts, and provide general administrative services."

In this chapter, you will find an overview of this very important aspect of business communications; but remember that it is just that—an overview. You know all too well that a single chapter or even a whole book will not make a computer expert of you. What it *will* do, however, is demystify the subject of computer skills and provide you with the ones you really need to do your job.

By the time you finish this chapter, you will have at least a speaking acquaintance with many of the ways your computer can help you do your job; several essential kinds of software and what they do; the basic terms used to describe computer hardware; the questions to ask yourself and the salesman before you buy a computer; the best way to set up your system, from taking it out of the carton to turning it on; and the functions, advantages, and disadvantages of important computer parts and peripherals.

Once Upon a Time

First, let's start with a very short history lesson. The computer on your desk probably looks no more complicated than a small box and a TV screen. But before this little phenomenon came to be, computers were so big they literally filled entire rooms. They were called *mainframes* then; and, for the most part, they stored data, performed amazingly complex calculations, and spit out reports that dazzled their operators. A smaller, but almost equally powerful version of the mainframe, is called a *minicomputer*; and, while both are still used all over the world, they are far outnumbered by their tiny successor—the *personal computer, or PC.*

The first real personal computer was born in a garage—the brainchild of Steve Jobs and Steve Wozniak—two young *techies* who changed the way we all function with their little invention. They called it the *Apple*; and the rest, as they say, is history. The Apple was followed by Apple II . . . then by IBM's much touted PC . . . then by countless IBM copies and clones . . . and, in 1984, by the first genuinely people-friendly computer—the Macintosh—complete with its revolutionary little mouse.

━━━━━━━━━━━━━━━━━━━━━━━━━━━━━━▶

Kathy Toennies, now a computer guru at Ideas to Images, met her first Macintosh at the advertising agency where she worked in word processing on an IBM-compatible PC.

"I had just been promoted to secretary in the public relations division. This was when Mac was very new. The agency had to do a whole book, so they bought a Mac and had somebody come in and teach two of us how to use it. That person gave us hands-on training every morning for two weeks. That's the best thing I could have asked for. Macs weren't very popular at that time; but the more I used them, the more I realized how marketable I was becoming. I had Mac experience, and there weren't that many other people out there who did. So, it was easy for me to get a new job. In every job I've had since then, I've known more about Macs than anyone there, except at this company. It's been a learning experience from day one."

━━━━━━━━━━━━━━━━━━━━━━━━━━━━━━▶

Chances are, you spend a bit of time with one of these incarnations of the personal computer. Up until recently you probably found yourself in either the PC camp or the Mac camp and thought never the twain would meet. PCs were run on an operating system called *DOS* and Macintoshes on an entirely different, not to mention incompatible, system of their own. You were either a PC person or a Mac person, but you couldn't be both. All that has changed, thanks to innovative software makers and a new, eminently sensible arrangement between IBM and Apple. You can now have the best of both worlds. The question you may be asking is, what do I do with it?

➤

Elnor Hickman is one of only 46,000 professional secretaries who have earned the designation of CPS—Certified Professional Secretary. Yet, even with these credentials and close to thirty years in the field, she laments her lack of opportunities to become as technologically proficient as she would like to be.

"I recently returned from our CPS seminar, where one of the sessions was on technology. I work for this small nonprofit, so our technology is not too sophisticated. With a nonprofit, funds, of course, are a real issue. It's unfortunate, but it's a part of the new reality. But to hear what people are actually using every day now . . . it is totally incredible. When our speaker called out the latest technologies and asked how many people were using them, I was amazed.

"If you work for an organization that is still not state-of-the-art, you are limited. Even if I were to go to a community college and take courses in the latest technology, if I didn't have an opportunity to use it every day, it would be totally worthless . . . time wasted. There is one thing I *can* do in this area, though. Executive secretaries do have the ear of their executives; and I continue to encourage our executive director, our administrator, and our MIS director to keep pressing the boundaries, so we don't get any further behind than we are. Some organizations are just miles ahead of others, and they could be two companies right across the street from each other."

➤

The Perfect Assistant

Let us assume that you are no newcomer to the world of computers. You probably use one every day, but perhaps you don't yet know all the things your computer could be helping you do. So, let's take a few minutes to explore its capabilities.

▶ First of all, your computer can *automate repetitive tasks for you*. If you have to write thirty letters that all say the same thing but go to thirty different people, you can cut your work time to a mere fraction of what it would be if you actually typed every letter individually. With a mail-merge option on your word processing program, you would type the text once, enter the list of names and addresses once, and program the computer to put them together in a perfect, personally addressed letter. Of course, you still have to stuff the envelopes and mail them, but maybe you could delegate that part of the job.

▶ The second thing your computer can do for you is *improve the accuracy of your work*. There are programs for everything—balancing checkbooks, doing payroll, calculating taxes, finding appropriate synonyms, checking spelling, and even advising you on grammar. No more calculators, dictionaries, thesauruses, or stylebooks. They're all built in.

▶ Third, your computer can *help you create professional-looking products all the time*. Not only will you produce flawless correspondence, you can also turn out graphs, tables, spreadsheets, reports, and even slick newsletters that look like they were created by professionals. Mistakes can be fixed in a flash; laser printers make everything look crisp; and, with the right equipment, you can even produce things in color.

▶ Fourth, your computer can *lighten your workload* by saving you time in countless ways. You can use it to do research without ever leaving your desk. You can combine sections of text from one file with columns of figures from another, illustrate both with graphics from a third, and assemble a dynamite report in record time. You can also calculate figures quickly, create sophisticated slides and overheads, save information and use it over and over in myriad ways, and automate just about any procedure you can think of.

▶ The fifth thing your computer can do for you is *broaden your horizons* through the contacts you make. Your computer may not be part of a network or attached to a mainframe, but be assured it does not exist in a vacuum. If you have a modem and a phone jack, you can link up with other computers, join an information service like CompuServe or America On Line, get around the Internet, send and receive e-mail messages, or hook up to a bulletin board that will put you in touch with other computer users.

The Hard Part: Software

It's difficult to believe that little box could do all that, isn't it? Well, quite honestly, it can't. That little box—whether it's an IBM, IBM-compatible, or a Mac—is your *hardware*. Technological marvel that it may be, it can't do a thing without the right *software*. Fortunately, there is software—or a computer program— for just about anything you might need to do in your job. Let's take a quick shopping trip through a typical software store and see what's available. We'll begin with the essentials. The one program you must have, and probably already use, is *word processing*. It's indispensable if you write letters, reports, books, brochures, memos, and anything else you used to type. It also helps you combine names and addresses with form letters, customize parts of those letters, and produce labels, to mention just a few of its functions.

If you maintain any kind of records or lists, you'll need a *database program* to keep track of all kinds of information— names, addresses, project details, inventory, and more. With database software, you can enter, organize, and print facts and figures exactly the way you want them to look.

---➤

Cindy Eastwood's only experience with computers was at a bank where she was employed as an operations manager. As the only administrative person in a busy office, she went to school to learn an entirely different type of software. Now, computers are her favorite part of the job.

"My role is to talk to candidates on the phone, initially, and to determine if their background and experience are in the same industries as those in which our account executives specialize. If so,

I ask them to send us their CV [curriculum vitae] by fax or mail; and, when I receive it, I enter that information into our database software, which is designed exclusively for our company. We have a unique situation here: we use a XENIX operating system, which is compatible with hardly anything else unless it has been specifically formatted for XENIX. As the business has grown, we've had to replace it with a new program so it would be more compatible with other systems."

➤

Assuming your responsibilities include manipulating numbers and planning, you'd better pick up a *spreadsheet program*, too. You'll need it when you're working with financial information, payroll, taxes, financial analyses, projections, or balance sheets. An absolute must for organizing you and your boss is a *project manager or scheduler.* With this type of program you can divide projects into parts, organize work flow, keep your calendar *and* your boss's up to date, and accomplish a host of other organizational activities.

Those are the programs you can't live without. Now let's move into the optional category, which puts at your fingertips the resources you need to expand your job about as far as you want it to go. Most of these have to do with visual effects of one kind or another. Artist or not, if you're finding yourself designing or laying out anything, one of the things you need on your software shelf is a *graphics package.*

➤

Patricia Diana started out in the financial industry and made a few moves before she landed at Bridge Information Systems. Along the way, she immersed herself in every opportunity to learn new software, from word processing and spreadsheets to complex graphics packages.

"At my last company, I worked on formatting, and I've been able to use those skills here. I have Harvard Graphics and AMI Pro software skills, as well. AMI Pro is comparable to Ventura, which is a publishing program; but it doesn't transfer well to Windows, which is a real problem. We also have a really great CC:Mail system here. When I need something, I can send a letter to our St. Louis office asking them for a document. They send the whole document back to me in the mail, and I can open it up on my screen and reformat it. Now it is a file on my computer, as well as theirs. There are a lot of programs out there. Every company has different ones. When you switch companies, as I have, you get this really great exposure to a variety of systems and software. I was interested in everything and learned as much as I could in every job."

━━━━━━━━━━━━━━━━━━━━━━━━━━━━━━━━▶

If you are really into highly specialized design—where you're creating plans, blueprints, and schematic drawings—you probably should think seriously about a *CAD,* or *computer-aided design,* package. Here's another question to ponder. Do you farm out the production of creative presentations to agencies or free lancers? You could do them yourself for a fraction of the cost with a *presentations graphic program* and have a lot of fun in the process. This software makes it easy to mix text and graphics for original and eye-catching visual effects.

Still in the optional category—but moving toward necessity—is the ability to link up with other computers, either in your own building or outside of it. To do this, you need *a phone line, a modem, and the communications software to run it;* and you are all set to talk to another computer across the country or around the world. A modem lets you get in touch with commercial mainframes and do research on virtually any subject. You can also tune into the latest news, plan your vacation, shop by computer, do your banking, communicate via e-mail, meet like-minded strangers, and even play games.

━━━━━━━━━━━━━━━━━━━━━━━━━━━━━━━━▶

Nancy Butler reports to the president and CEO of a multinational corporation. At home with transatlantic communications of all kinds, she admits e-mail can make life much easier. On the other hand . . .

"I have a pet peeve: electronic mail. Data communication is wonderful. It's a great tool, but it has some disadvantages, too. We've become so automated, we tend to send notes, rather than making that personal contact. I've seen it happen in our company. We forget the *real* method of communication—verbal communication—and the value of the personal relationships that develop from that.

"On the plus side, it's a time-saver for those who are sending the messages. E-mail is very reliable. Here, we use it internationally, as well as internally, because our parent company is in Europe; and it helps with the time difference. The downside is that it's not always very efficient. If you need to resolve an issue, and you're going to be going back and forth with messages, it's a lot better to get on the phone and work it out personally. It takes a conscious effort in judgment to know when to use the phone and when to use e-mail."

Speaking of *games*, they happen to be big business and PC-compatible. You can buy software for puzzles, mysteries, cards, and more leisure activities than you can imagine. Except for stress reduction, though, it is difficult to consider this a must-have package for your job.

Finally, under the optional heading, is software that helps you teach yourself or others. Used in schools, at home, and in the training departments of many companies, *educational software* is a fast and efficient way to learn anything from accounting to another language. For secretaries, it is truly a job-enhancement tool.

Deciphering Computereze

While this quick tour of essential and not-so-essential software packages won't necessarily make you an expert, at least it will give you some grounding in the *software* side of the equation. For most people, though, it is the *hardware* that strikes fear in the heart and stupor in the mind. Computers are described in language that bears little resemblance to English. If you wanted to buy one, without a degree in computer science, you might find it an intimidating experience. Imagine, for a moment that you want to purchase a new computer. You haven't decided between a PC and a Mac, so you comb through descriptive material for both. It's a safe bet that some of the terminology in the material leaves you confused and feeling like you're comparing apples to cantaloupes.

If most of what you read is Greek to you, be comforted by knowing it is to most novice computer shoppers. For that reason, computer expert and author Danny Goodman has translated this typical computer lingo for us in his extremely user-friendly book called *Fear Computers No More*. Borrowing from his explanations, we are going to do some basic translation of key terminology:

Let's say you are browsing through two pieces of computer literature. One is for an IBM or IBM-compatible personal computer; the other describes a Macintosh. You put them next to each other, hoping to compare them point by point and then make an intelligent purchasing decision. You run into trouble immediately.

▶ The PC is called a *486 DX*—a bit impersonal, but actually a pretty informative name. The Macintosh's name is *IIci*, which doesn't tell you much, at least not yet. PCs all have numbers for names, and those numbers refer to the most important single element in the computer—the *microprocessor chip*—another word for *brains*. PCs have evolved over the years from 286's to 386's to 486's and now to 586's.

▶ The mysterious list of features that follows the computer's name also provides a lot of information, *if* you can break the code. Both machines, you read, are 33 *MHz*. MHz stands for megahertz, which is a measure of speed. A 33 MHz is a pretty fast computer. So, you know that these two computers will operate at the same speed. No winner there.

▶ The PC number 80486 and the Mac number 68030 stand for the microprocessor chip. PCs use the 8000 series of these chips; Mac uses a different model, called the 6800 series. How do they compare? The 486 is near the top of the line, while a 68030 Mac is considered mid-range. That means the PC is the "higher-end" computer of the two. Advantage PC.

▶ The next mystery word is *RAM*. Whatever it means, this particular computer PC has four, and the Mac has five. What's the difference? RAM is an acronym for *random-access memory*, which is what the computer uses to store software programs and the work you do while the computer is turned on. Microprocessors and RAM are both chips, but they do different jobs. The microprocessing chip does the *thinking*; the RAM chip is in charge of *storage*. The more RAM your computer has, the more programs you can run at the same time and the faster you can work. *4M RAM* means you can store 4 million bytes of information; 5M means you can store 5 million bytes. (A byte is roughly equivalent to one word of information.) The Mac moves out ahead on this feature.

▸ Both the PC and the Macintosh have a 212 *hard disk* or *hard drive*. First, let's clarify that the words *drive* and *disk* in this context are interchangeable. They are storage devices inside the computer that maintain programs and data, even after you turn the equipment off. And these two will both hold up to 212 million bytes of information, which is quite a bit. As software programs have increased in size and variety, computer hard drives have, of necessity, gotten correspondingly larger, too. Today, 120M is the norm; so with 212M, you'd be in pretty good shape.

▸ The PC has *six expansion slots*, which simply means you can add six different capabilities to your computer in the future, as your needs change. It also offers *dual, or two*, floppy drives—which are just another way of storing your programs and data. Floppy drives aren't really floppy; they are external, and you insert disks into them. External disk drives come in two sizes to accommodate 3^1/$_2$-inch and 5^1/$_4$-inch disks. Most PCs have one of each because IBM-compatible disks come in two sizes. Macs, on the other hand, only use the smaller size disk.

▸ We're almost to the end of the list. The PC boasts 512K *video RAM*, which is one of the newer developments in hardware. Video RAM is special memory included on the video adapter—the device inside your computer that sends the picture to the screen. Not all computers offer video RAM; this particular model of the Mac does not. If you're really into bells and whistles, you would probably chalk up another point for the PC on this feature.

▸ Now we get to *monitors*, otherwise known as *viewing screens*. Monitors come in a variety of shapes and sizes, including portrait, landscape, full page, two page, and oversized. The PC boasts an ultra *VGA monitor*. VGA is the current standard, but the descriptive material doesn't tell you what size it is. The Mac's has a 14-inch monitor, but you don't know anything about its shape or capabilities. So, neither one gets a point on this one.

▶ That's it for the PC, but the Mac has two more items on its list: a *cache card* and a Key Tronic MacPro Plus *extended keyboard*. A *cache* is a special portion of memory that runs off a few high-speed memory chips—different from those chips used for RAM—and can significantly speed up the computer's processing capabilities. An extended keyboard is longer and more complex than a standard keyboard, contains a number keypad that works like a calculator, and is equipped with a set of function keys. This adds two points to the Mac's scorecard.

Karen Brunner, CPRW, launched her secretarial business with a typewriter. Her first computer was an IBM PC, which she sold to buy a more "user-friendly" Macintosh. She found she could still deliver the same quality with a Mac, yet learn the programs much more quickly. Karen now owns a Mac Power PC, which gives her the best of both worlds.

"I own a full-service secretarial service. I work out of my home, and most of my clients come to my office. Just keeping up with the technology and learning the latest upgrades of all the programs is a job in itself. My company provides general secretarial services, as well as medical transcription, desktop publishing, editing and proofreading, repetitive letters, mailing services, bulk mail, notary public services, spreadsheets, and databases. I have an OCR and image scanner and a modem. I am also a Certified Professional Resume Writer."

Six of One, Half Dozen of Another?

Where does all that leave you besides a little more conversant in computereze than you were before? Which hardware should you buy? The choice of a PC versus a Macintosh depends, not on which one got the most points (the PC won by one point, by the way) but which one best meets *your* needs. This means you have to do some serious thinking about what your needs are and how they might evolve over time. As an exercise, try answering these questions:

1. What size and type of computer are you looking for—desktop, laptop, or palmtop?
2. How fast do you want it to be?
3. How much memory do you think you'll need—4 or 5 RAM or more? (The answer is probably more.)
4. How much storage room do you need on your hard drive—120M, 212M, or more?
5. Is it important to you to be able to upgrade this machine in the future? If so, how many expansion slots might that take?
6. Will you need both size floppy drives, or are you going to use only the $3^1/_2$ inch disks?
7. Do you really need a state-of-the-art monitor and video capabilities?
8. Do you want to speed up your computer processing capabilities with a cache card?
9. And, finally, what are you going to use your keyboard for?

It's not too likely you'll be able to answer all those questions immediately. How much memory and hard-drive storage space you want will depend on how many programs you're planning to run and how big those programs are. If your job requires a lot of graphics software, you can be sure you'll need more hard-drive space than if you're only planning to use word processing and scheduling programs.

If every question leads to five more, don't be discouraged. It's just time to refine your needs a little more. If, for example, you know you want to view a complete letter on your screen, just as it will look when it's printed, you would probably prefer a full-page monitor. If you do newsletters, you might opt for a two-page. If spreadsheets are your main focus, consider the landscape format. The key is to make a list of the features that will help you do what *your job* requires. If you never design or lay out anything, you probably don't need a desktop publishing package, which would require a lot of space and memory. If numbers are a big part of your responsibilities, you might consider that extended keyboard with the handy number pad right at your fingertips.

Cathy Boyer, a pathology secretary, has a computer that is, as she puts it, "compatible with almost nothing." She uses it to enter patient information, generate reports, send bills, collect specimens, and retrieve data. Up until recently, her department's operating system wasn't even compatible with the one the rest of the hospital was using.

"Computers are not new to me. I've been through eight major computer transitions, starting with mainframes. It is just a matter of what you get used to. When you use something daily, you get used to it real fast. When I started this job, they had what I would call a *dinosaur*; but they've come up to the nineties.

"It's hard to stay current because the computer industry is two years ahead; every time you buy something, there's something new coming out. We're currently involved in going from two separate computer systems to a consolidated one that includes word processing, report generating, and data-retrieval capabilities. This is for the Pathology Department only. Our hospital made this transition two years ago. Pathology is just now getting into their system. It's been a *very* slow process."

Here are a few very basic questions to ask yourself or the computer salesperson before you sign on the dotted line and suddenly find yourself with a permanent roommate you don't particularly like:

▸ Question one: Do you like the way the keyboard feels? That includes the touch and sound of the keys, the shape of the board, and how your hands and wrists are positioned while you're using it.

▶ Question two: Is the monitor adequate for everyday use—the right size, the right shape, the right height, the proper brightness?

▶ Question three: Does the computer run the software you need?

▶ Question four: Does the system have enough memory to run the programs you want to run?

Assembling the Hardware Puzzle

We won't pretend that buying a computer is a snap if you can answer those four questions or that you won't suffer a twinge or two of buyer's remorse after the fact. But in the interest of time and space, let's say you have made a decision. You chose one or the other, or some hybrid of the two like a Macintosh Power PC, which attempts to mesh the best of both worlds. You own this thing—or at least your company owns it—and you are its custodian.

Now what? Assuming that this is a new system, the way in which you arrange it in your work space has a lot to do with your comfort while you use it. If you put it somewhere where it's difficult to use, it isn't going to help you do your job; it's just going to be a nuisance. Computer equipment can be bulky and hard to organize, especially if you have many different wires stretching all over the place. Take some time to think about where things might go, visualize what it will look like, and then allow yourself to change your mind if it doesn't work for you. If your computer isn't new, you might seriously consider rearranging its components after you read this chapter.

Begin by placing your *system unit*—the computer box—so the *power switch* is on the side you can reach most easily. Make sure the *computer reset button* or *on/off switch* is not in a place where you can bump it accidentally and obliterate your last two hours of work. Be sure, too, that you can insert and remove floppy disks easily. If your computer is a *tower system unit*—meaning it stands on one end, vertically instead of horizontally—you may want to put it under your desk, instead of on top of it. If you do have a tower system and have opted for the desk, our advice is, do get a *tower stand*. A fall from your desk to the floor is a guaranteed death sentence for your system unit, no matter how hearty it is.

This may sound too obvious to mention, but we will anyway. Put the system near an electrical outlet so you have a place to plug in all those power cords. Most systems have more power cords than a single electrical outlet can handle, meaning that you will probably need a *surge protector*. This is a specially designed strip of outlets that accommodates up to ten plugs and absorbs unexpected electrical power surges or spikes.

This collection of boxes and screens and keyboards can take up a lot of room—room you probably need for other kinds of work. Even though the computer age was supposed to give us a paperless world, that just didn't happen. You still produce, accumulate, read, process, and file a lot of paper; and you will need some desk space on which to do those things. If your computer has a *mouse*—which is likely with either a Mac or a PC— put it on in the right side of the computer if you're right-handed and on the left side if you're left-handed. Also, make sure the mouse cord is not squeezed tight or wound around anything.

While you certainly have to be able to reach your phone, it's a good idea to move the phone *away* from the computer system and any loose floppy disks that happen to be on your desk. A telephone is a magnetic field. It can erase or damage disks (another good reason to set up a separate phone center). Also, it's probably not the only magnetic culprit in your office. Even a paper-clip holder can be a menace.

Obviously, you will be staring into your *monitor* for a good portion of your workday. There are several things you can do to minimize the stress and strain of that arrangement. For one, make sure the light source is good enough to do the rest of your work, but not so bright that you can't see your monitor. For another, try to place your monitor at eye level. To do that, you may have to adjust your desk, chair, or monitor height— whichever is easiest. Third, put the monitor in a well-ventilated place. Monitors have vents on their sides, back, or top to permit heated air to escape. If you put it on a shelf or against a wall, blocking the airflow, it may fry.

The last piece of equipment you have to place is your *printer*. Fortunately, this is the one that gives you the most flexibility because it doesn't have to be right next to the rest of the system. On the other hand, it does have to be close enough to connect, and that will depend on the length of the printer cable. You'll also want to check that the paper can move freely through the printer and to think about where it will go after it's printed. If it's onto a tray, fine; if it's piling up on the floor or obstructing the paper flow in some way, not so fine.

One last chunk of advice on setup—*the don'ts*, according to computer guru Danny Goodman:

- ▸ Don't string cables in front of your computer, except for the keyboard and mouse cable, which should run along one side of the system unit.
- ▸ Don't position a desk lamp so it shines on the monitor.
- ▸ Don't put a regular system unit on its side like a tower unit.
- ▸ Don't push the system all the way back against the wall or so far toward the front of the desktop that the keyboard slides off the desk into your lap.
- ▸ Don't stack things on your monitor.
- ▸ Don't keep your refreshment center next to your computer.

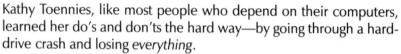

Kathy Toennies, like most people who depend on their computers, learned her do's and don'ts the hard way—by going through a hard-drive crash and losing *everything*.

"Everything from the last year was just wiped out. I had a backup on the accounting program, and that was it. If there's any message here, it's to back up at least once a week, if not every night. You can overload your computer by putting so much junk on it that you don't need. In a way, losing my whole hard drive was a blessing, because it forced me to start over and load only what I actually needed. I reloaded Quark Express, Pagemaker, Photo Shop, Illustrator—all graphics programs—plus FileMaker, Excel, and Quicken —my database, spreadsheet, and accounting programs. The rest had just been cluttering up my hard drive."

Down to Details

Finally, we're going to touch briefly on some of the finer points you don't want to learn the hard way. Let's start with *floppy disks*, which are notorious for going bad, especially the $5^1/4$ inch variety. One minute they're fine; the next they're dead, and so is all your work. Floppy disks get old. They get dirty. They get erased by anything magnetic. And, of course, they get full. They also get sick and are particularly prone to viruses—some, fairly benign and some, downright murderous. If the virus is virulent, it can eat away your most important files and then go on to munch on your hard drive. So, rule #1 is get a virus detection program. Rule #2 is don't ever accept a disk from any one you don't know. And rule #3 is never use an inherited disk without running it through your virus detector.

Next on our tour of finer points is your *keyboard*, which is probably the most undervalued accoutrement to your computer system. Your keyboard, believe it or not, can be your friend or your nemesis. That's why it's so important to determine *before* you commit whether the keys feel right, if the layout of keys makes sense for your needs, whether the shape of the board fits the shape of your hands, and if your hands and wrists are comfortable when you type.

Keyboards have personalities and idiosyncrasies, according to Goodman. Some have spring-touch keys that meet your fingers as soon as you press on them. Others make clicks when you type that can range from barely audible to loud enough to drive you crazy. Some keyboards stick on certain letters and just keep repeating them. Others can render the same letter invisible, but only temporarily. When you least expect it, the recalcitrant letter will suddenly reappear. Keyboards aren't terribly expensive; but if one goes out on you, it could cost you more to fix it than to replace it.

Something else that has a personality all its own is your *monitor*, which is your link to the computer system. Since you spend so much time staring at the monitor, the quality of its display is obviously very important. If your monitor is not at eye level, and you can't fix it by raising or lowering anything, you might consider buying a separate monitor stand that will put it at the right height. *Where* you sit in relation to the monitor matters, too, in terms of cramped muscles and eyestrain. Monitors are relatively low maintenance *if* you follow these basic common-sense guidelines:

- ▸ Keep all liquids as far away from it as possible.
- ▸ Make sure it is adequately ventilated.
- ▸ Turn it off or use a screen-saver program when you're not using your computer.
- ▸ Every so often, check to see that the cable and power cord are tight.
- ▸ Fill out and turn in the warranty card that comes with the monitor.

Another fine point is that little *mouse* no one ever heard of before Macintosh introduced it in 1984 and which has since become virtually indispensable. The mouse allows you to point to things on the computer screen, select the item you want, and do something with it. This speeds things up considerably. But mice are sensitive little creatures. They stick. Things stick to them. They get disconnected. Now and then, they play dead. Sometimes, they aren't playing.

The penultimate fine point is your *printer*. Obviously, different kinds of printers produce different kinds of output. Dot matrix printers are fast and slow, but inexpensive. Their other disadvantage is that everything printed on them is in a pattern of dots. While the quality is not always wonderful, if you want a reliable, fast, and economical workhorse, this is your printer. Letter-quality printers are a step up from dot matrix but not in the same league with lasers. Laser printers deliver high quality and fast output but for a higher price tag.

Making a comeback are thermal transfer and inkjet printers that are benefiting from greatly improved technology. Thermal transfer printers create characters and graphics by melting a wax-based ink off a ribbon and pressing it onto the page. They provide good resolution, quiet printing, and interesting effects for color printing. Inkjet printers create the printed page by spraying characters and graphics in a pattern of ink dots. The printers uses ink cartridges instead of a ribbon or toner for high-resolution though slow printing.

Susan Beal is in charge of quality control at Eagle Brands, one of the de la Cruz Companies, in Miami. A big part of her job revolves around computers, where she does a little bit of everything, from ordering new ones to fixing troublesome ones. To her, "computers are wonderful." Here are some of Susan's suggestions for keeping them that way.

"Put a protective screen on the front of your monitor. A protective screen softens the lighting, helps protects your eyes, and flattens the image a little bit. The screen doesn't have to be really high. In fact, you should place it a little lower so you can look down at it. Use a screen saver, so you don't keep everything on your screen in the exact same position. Otherwise, the color pixels will bore right into your screen; and you'll keep that picture on there forever.

"Use a wrist guard; and keep your keyboard down low on a pull-out drawer or shelf, if possible. Your chair should be very comfortable and provide back support. I usually put my tower underneath my desk, but not where I can knock it with my knee and turn if off or reset it. Check your mouse to be sure it's clean underneath where the ball is. Having a little pad there helps keep it clean. You should also clean your computer once a year, if not every six months. Just pull off the cover, and use a computer air pressure cleaner. Once you learn how, you can do it yourself. But even if you don't want to open the computer, you can still clean the back. Make sure all the cables are hooked up tightly. Always plug the computer into a power surge protector; and, in a storm, keep it turned off."

Last but not least on our list of fine points are those tools that enhance even the best system—*modems, scanners, and faxes.* If you think of your computer as a communications center, you will see how indispensable these three additions to your system can become:

▸ A *modem* is an electronic device that uses the phone lines to send and receive data to and from other computers, thus linking you to computers around the corner or around the world. Modems come in two varieties: *external and internal.* An external unit is placed outside the system unit of your computer; the internal one fits inside and plugs into the motherboard. Modems are multifaceted; they can be used to transfer files back and forth . . . to leave messages in an electronic mailbox . . . to talk to other computer users . . . and to access huge commercial databases, information services, and the Internet. The modem definitely puts you in touch with the world in a way you never dreamed of.

▸ *Scanners* turn something on paper—text or art—into data and convert that into a computer file. The scanner and its accompanying software literally *read* what's on the page, transfer that information to your computer, and save the scanned image in a file you can access like any other file in your system. There are several kinds of scanners, including handheld, half-page, flat-bed, and drum, each with its own particular advantages. Handheld scanners are about twice as big as the mouse and cover a little less than half a page. They do a great job on small images like logos, but don't work too well on large ones. Half-page scanners are really large hand scanners that can scan a half-page at a time. They tend to wobble when held. Flat-bed scanners are like copiers but smaller. The item to be scanned is placed under a cover, on glass, and scanned into the computer in gray scales or color. Drums are the most sophisticated and, consequently, the most expensive.

▸ Finally, there are *faxes*, which are becoming as essential to the business of doing business as telephones. There are two kinds of faxes: *stand-alones*, which are separate machines, and *fax boards* that go inside your computer. The stand-alone fax can have all sorts of special features, like speed dial, a fax telephone, and copy capability. The fax board, on the other hand, allows you to save the received file as computer data you can then use in other applications. Stand-alone faxes can be expensive, ranging from $500 on up, especially if you get one that prints on plain paper. Fax boards, surprisingly, are less expensive. The average cost for a fax board is between $250 and $400.

Ideas to Images, Kathy Toennies's company, is "a retail image management group that specializes in electronic prepress and print services." As such, it is a business that is highly dependent on sophisticated technology. One example is the modem that connects Kathy to her clients' computers.

"We have a high-end modem, but it's pretty much dedicated to one client. It's on all the time, because we never know when that client is going to send data. To access it, someone would also have to have a high-end modem, which uses special phone lines to transfer data so much faster than can be done on regular phone lines."

Staying Healthy

There is one more important point to make about computers: they *can* be dangerous to your health—if you misuse your equipment and abuse your body. Computer-related disorders (CRDs) range from eyestrain to carpal tunnel syndrome and all points in between. The most effective way to deal with them is to prevent them from happening in the first place. Some changes, such as special chairs or keyboards, may cost your employer a little money; but there are many improvements you can make that will cost little or nothing. Here are a few suggestions from an old issue of *Macworld*, a magazine for Macintosh users:

▶ *Chair:* Choose a chair you tailor to suit your body. It should have multiple adjustment points that allow you to sit back all the way against your chair back and to move your knees and lower legs freely.

▶ *Work Surface:* Try to find a work surface that is appropriate for your body size and will provide ample work area for your monitor, keyboard, and other peripherals. There should be at least two inches of clearance between the tops of your thighs and the underside of the desktop or keyboard tray. A pull-out keyboard tray is helpful. You should not have to stretch to use your mouse or trackball.

▶ *Keyboards:* Because keyboards are considered a prime contributor to CRDs, it's a good idea to look for the following features—a comfortable level of resistance; some auditory or tactile feedback when you touch the keys; an adjustable angle or tilt; function keys to help cut down on the number of keystrokes; and a separate, movable numeric keypad.

▶ *Pads and Braces:* Wrist pads and other add-ons offer inexpensive solutions to some of the deficiencies in keyboards. Padded wrist rests that sit in front the keyboard are widely used, but be careful *not* to brace your wrists on them while you're typing. That added pressure may actually increase the risk of CRDs.

▶ *Pointing Devices:* The mouse and trackball are the two most common pointing devices. There are also joysticks and pens. Each has its own special uses and potential for injury. The important thing is to choose one that feels comfortable to you and that works for the type of work you do. A mouse should fit comfortably in your cupped hand. A trackball should move easily, but not too easily. Its buttons should be easy to reach and press and should provide adequate feedback when pushed.

▶ *Monitor:* Eyestrain and headaches are two hazards associated with staring at your monitor for long periods of time. To prevent it, your monitor's height should be adjustable so that the top of the visible screen is just below eye level. It should swivel to help get rid of annoying reflections. The display should be sharp enough to read without staining your eyes and bright enough to match the ambient lighting.

▶ *Lighting:* The environment in which you work is very important, and even small changes can have a major impact on your comfort level. The lighting in your work area should be balanced. Try to avoid glare and bright spots. If your overhead or other lights are too bright and cause reflections, you can make an inexpensive cardboard shield for your monitor, wear an eyeshade, remove a couple of light bulbs, or simply change the angle of the light.

▶ *Air Comfort:* Secondhand smoke is only one example of poor air quality that can make you sick. Not so obvious are ways in which other conditions such as temperature and humidity can affect you health. For most people, a working temperature of about 69 degrees F is ideal. High or low humidity can be uncomfortable. Low humidity can cause symptoms like dry eyes, nose, and mouth. This is especially troublesome to contact lens wearers.

▶ *Noise:* Whether it is the constant hum of a disk drive, the ringing of telephones, or the incessant chattering of a co-worker at the next desk, noise works on your stress level. You can cut noise levels by placing offending equipment on the floor; requesting padded partitions to muffle noise in adjacent areas; or, if necessary, wearing earplugs.

Summing Up

Computers are playing an ever more important role in your ability to do, much less excel at, your job. In the broad realm of communications, mastery of that machine on your desk is a nonnegotiable skill. You *must* have it. In this chapter, you saw all the reasons why you would *want* to have it, from lightening your workload to broadening your contact base. You took a quick tour of necessary-to-optional software and the primary functions of each, translated the strange descriptive terminology of hardware, walked through the assembly of a new computer system and some of the subtler aspects of your computer system, and finished up with a list of suggestions on minimizing computer-related injuries and illness.

This chapter focused on your relationship with technology; the next and final one shifts gears back to the human dimension and plunges into the myriad of skills it takes to plan, implement, manage, and conduct meetings.

Chapter 8

Meetings:
Your Living Laboratory

Meetings, it seems, are the subject of a love-hate relationship. On one hand, they provide a critical link in the chain of communication in every organization. Fulfilling a multiplicity of purposes, they are integral to the way business is conducted and information communicated. On the other hand, they are the least favorite activities for those who conduct or attend them, a group that includes almost everybody who works. As your responsibilities continue to grow in scope and complexity, meetings inevitably play an ever larger part in what you do. You may be already involved in planning, organizing, arranging for, taking notes at, and following up on meetings. But beyond these traditional roles, it is conceivable that you will eventually find yourself in the role of meeting leader.

Secretaries, these days, are expected to be meeting planners, public relations experts, and special event coordinators—all of which require a unique set of meeting-related communications skills. That is precisely why there is a whole chapter devoted to them. By the time you finish reading it, you will understand why meetings often fail to achieve their intended purposes and how to plan an effective meeting, prepare for the most common preventable problems that can derail even the best-planned meetings, and defuse the land mines that can blow up when least expected. You'll also have a handle on the key elements of effective meeting management and on the importance of taking every meeting through the wrap-up and evaluation stages.

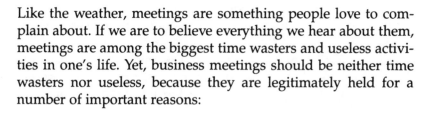

Cathy Boyer wears a lot of hats as pathology secretary for a large hospital. Her constituencies range from physicians to living and deceased patients. Her responsibilities are equally varied, running the gamut from medical staff meetings to postmortem examinations.

"I'm the person in the background who coordinates all of the meetings. We have one once a month called the *tumor board*. This is when all the doctors meet in the lounge to discuss different types of cancers. The bottom line of what we do is distinguish malignant from nonmalignant. I assist in some of the autopsies that take place. I'm kind of a diener/secretary/receptionist, all rolled into one. A *diener* is someone who actually assists doctors with autopsies—not quite a pathology assistant, but someone who can get around the body in a very basic way."

Like the weather, meetings are something people love to complain about. If we are to believe everything we hear about them, meetings are among the biggest time wasters and useless activities in one's life. Yet, business meetings should be neither time wasters nor useless, because they are legitimately held for a number of important reasons:

- ▶ To exchange ideas
- ▶ To identify and solve problems
- ▶ To define roles and responsibilities
- ▶ To promote creative thinking
- ▶ To convey information
- ▶ To motivate, inspire, and teach
- ▶ To establish and communicate policy
- ▶ To encourage commitment
- ▶ To make decisions

Gordon Graham & Co. is a "lean, mean organization" with a few full-time employees, all of whom wear several hats. To be sure nothing slips between the cracks, Katie Olney, who is often the liaison between the staff and the boss, attends weekly staff meetings.

"We have interoffice meetings every week to talk about what is going on with each of us and where we may need some help, if one of us is in the middle of a project. We keep each other posted and just talk in general about what we are involved in. When Gordy is in town, he likes to go over everything with everybody—do a kind of rundown on what's going on with all major clients and what we've done about touching bases with all of our facilitators. We want our facilitators to feel like they're an extension of our company, so we contact them regularly by phone and by mail."

The Bane of Everyone's Existence

With such lofty, not to mention pragmatic, reasons for having meetings you'd think someone would figure out how to make them do what they were designed to do. Yet, they are as unpopular as they are inevitable and often as unproductive as they are predictable.

The question, of course, is *why*? The answer is multifaceted. First, people tend to get what they expect. And when they expect meetings to waste their time, achieve little or nothing, and put them to sleep, that is often just what happens. Second, meetings are nothing more than a reflection of the management style of the organization as a whole. If top management encourages an open exchange of ideas and opinions, meetings will probably be spirited and candid. If, on the other hand, top management runs a tight ship, meeting leaders will follow that lead and run relatively uptight meetings.

Third, a great many meetings lack purpose. No one knows why they are there. The objective of the meeting is never announced or questioned. The discussion rambles from topic to topic. Issues are raised, but not resolved. Problems are aired, but never solved. And people leave feeling confused or frustrated.

Kathy Pierce's involvement with meetings depends on who she is working for at the moment. With one state representative, she "makes the meetings" (organizes them and ensures that every one who needs to be there *is* there) but rarely attends them.

"We make and break meetings frequently, especially during session. When I'm making a meeting between January and April, I always tell the person on the other end, 'I will call and confirm on the day of the meeting.' Every meeting is contingent on the representatives not being called to a caucus, not having to go to the floor, or not having something unexpected come up. They just don't have a real firm schedule when session is in; and, in March and April, it really gets hairy.

"I would say the majority of the meetings I'm involved in are very worthwhile. Very few meetings are just to provide an update on what has been happening. The majority of the meetings are informative and have a definite purpose and a definite time frame, so they don't go on all day. Most of them do achieve their purposes. Sometimes it takes three or four meetings to get to that point, but there is usually an outcome, eventually."

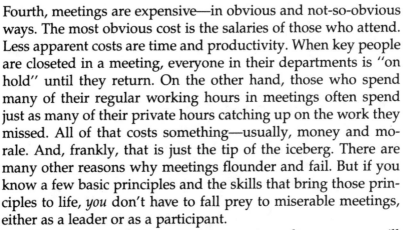

Fourth, meetings are expensive—in obvious and not-so-obvious ways. The most obvious cost is the salaries of those who attend. Less apparent costs are time and productivity. When key people are closeted in a meeting, everyone in their departments is "on hold" until they return. On the other hand, those who spend many of their regular working hours in meetings often spend just as many of their private hours catching up on the work they missed. All of that costs something—usually, money and morale. And, frankly, that is just the tip of the iceberg. There are many other reasons why meetings flounder and fail. But if you know a few basic principles and the skills that bring those principles to life, *you* don't have to fall prey to miserable meetings, either as a leader or as a participant.

What can you do as a participant, since chances are you'll often find yourself in that position? If you don't like the way things are going, you have three options: you can accept and adjust; you can change it; or you can leave. Each has its risks and its rewards, which only you can weigh. One thing you do have control over and can change is the way *you* are doing things. If you're talking too much, let others speak. If you're contributing nothing, concentrate and speak up occasionally. In other words, whatever you're doing, try the opposite.

Elnor Hickman is a rare exception to the rule—a person who unabashedly *loves* meetings. As president of Professional Secretaries International (PSI), she has, of course, presided over many of them through the years.

"PSI has so many meetings, they are not the bane of our existence at all. They are the foundation of what we're about. We have many publications, and we communicate all the time, every day. But when we come together at meetings, *that's* when we are able to communicate most effectively. We are specialists in the meeting business. We had over 400 people at our CPS seminar, 400 at our student meeting in Memphis, and over 1,300 registered so far for our international conference in Seattle. One of the things that makes our meetings work so well is that we have twenty-eight staff people at our headquarters in Kansas City, Missouri; and though our officers change every year, that staff remains the same. There's continuity . . . there is great depth of experience there."

When *You* Run the Meeting

Now let's shift gears and make this assumption: *you* have been asked to conduct a meeting. From start to finish, this is your baby. The first question is, where do you begin? And the answer is, long before the day of the meeting. The secret of effective meetings is what goes on before the fact, and that is called *planning*. Good meetings don't just happen; they are choreographed. Often, in fact, more work is done before the meeting than during it. And planning is something you already do very well. So, how do you apply what you do naturally to this new assignment? As you will see, there are seven steps to planning for effective meetings, and they are very logical.

1. *Define your objective.* In other words, ask yourself what you hope to accomplish at this meeting; and answer that question in terms of results or outcomes.

2. *Select the right participants.* Who should be at this meeting? That will depend, of course, on your meeting's objective. But here are a few rules of thumb. Invite people who have some stake in the outcome . . . people who have something to contribute or to gain from the discussion . . . people who have a need and right to hear the information you're presenting . . . people who will implement the policy you'll be discussing . . . people who must make the necessary decisions . . . and people who are creative and innovative thinkers.

3. *Decide when to hold your meeting.* Select a time when both you and your attendees will be available and when you will have enough time to cover your subject. *When* also means day or night, before work, during work, or after work. Will a daytime meeting keep key people tied up or carve out a huge chunk of their workday? Or will an evening meeting interfere with their time with their families? Which would they prefer? Which do *you* prefer?

4. *Draft an agenda.* An agenda is a way to tell participants what topics you plan to cover and how much time you are allotting to each topic. It's also a very useful tool for you because it helps you organize every aspect of your meeting: topics, speakers, visual aids, props, group involvement, and anything else you might choose to include. An agenda is your working plan and, as such, it should be flexible enough to meet your changing needs.

5. *Choose a site, and make the physical arrangements.* This could be as simple as reserving the conference room and arranging for coffee or as complicated as booking a four-day meeting out of town. The most important single criterion for choosing a site is to think of your meeting as "a human event" (a phrase coined by meeting expert Richard J. Dunsing) and select a setting fit for humans. That means it should be clean, well ventilated, will lit, well organized, and comfortable. Beyond these basics, you should consider the following:

- ► Location (on site or off)
- ► The size of the room (office, conference room, or auditorium)
- ► Availability of equipment
- ► Seating arrangements
- ► Suitable amenities

If all of that sounds a little overwhelming, just remember that the key to choosing a meeting site is that it must always move you toward your objective and meet the needs of your participants.

6. *Notify the participants.* Do you do this in person or in writing? Do you do it well in advance or closer to the date of your meeting? Do you send materials and an agenda ahead of time or present them when you meet? The answers, once again, flow from your objective. What do you hope to achieve, and what is the best way to do that? Once you decide, you'll automatically know the answers to these questions.

7. *Make the final preparations.* This is your last chance to minimize glitches and unpleasant surprises. Rule number one is "don't assume anything," and by that we mean *anything* at all. Rule number two, just in case you did, is "check and double-check everything"; and by that we mean absolutely *everything*. And that, in a nutshell, is the meeting planning process—the seven stepping-stones to good preparation.

━━━━━━━━━━━━━━━━━━━━━━━━━━━━━━━━▶

Linda Yaniszewski, president of Executive Secretarial Services, is a big believer in meetings, agendas, and brainstorming. She has learned meeting skills "by the seat of her pants" and by searching for "a better way" when something doesn't go well. To Linda, the key to a successful meeting comes *after* the meeting, when the action list is implemented.

"We have a staff meeting every Monday morning and a team leader meeting once a month. We work hard to keep the lines of communication open, so our people will go to their team leaders with problems or suggestions. The team leaders, in turn, bring those issues to our meeting. At our staff meetings, we try to encourage everyone to offer their ideas and recommendations. We do what we can to draw them out to express their frustrations and recommendations. We are very limited on time; it's hard to get the whole staff together. I try to hold those meetings from 7:30 to 9:00 in the morning and to bring breakfast in. I think agendas are very important. I'm also very sensitive to timing. If it looks like we're spending way too much time on a certain topic, we note that in the meeting. The key, of course, is making sure the things decided in the meeting actually get done after the meeting.

"Anything we've done that has made a significant impact on the business—whether it relates to new profit centers, client growth, or any other subject—has all been stimulated at meetings with my staff and the brainstorming we do at those meetings. Working to listen to their ideas and their suggestions has really helped me to grow the business."

Looking back on her experience as a meeting leader, Elnor Hickman describes the process as "learning the basics, then fine-tuning."

"I started with this organization (PSI) at the chapter level, then served as a chapter officer and a chapter president for two years. That's where I learned the basics. In addition to having regular chapter meetings, most chapters hold events throughout the year; and I gained experience in planning and leading these different types of meetings. Actually, once I got the basics, the meetings just became *larger and more sophisticated.* In Chicago, we dealt with one part of Chicago. In the divisions, we dealt with the entire state. When I became an international director, I was responsible for meetings that involved five states. Over the years, I have learned from experience what works, what does not work, what I want to try again, and what I don't want to try again."

Sound like a lot of work for one little meeting? Perhaps. But suppose you had neglected to do it. Imagine all the disasters that might have ensued. This way, at least, you were prepared. So, does that mean that planning will guarantee a trouble-free meeting? Unfortunately, it doesn't. Even the best-planned meeting can go awry. The four most likely derailers of even a well-orchestrated meeting are lack of structure, runaway discussions, abdicating control, and forgetting to close. Let's look at each of them.

Sue St. John has been conducting meetings ever since her first supervisory position. Over the years she has learned a great deal, especially about planning. The secret, she says, is to keep focused.

"When I define my meeting's purpose, I find it more productive to keep it to one or two major issues, rather than a shopping list of objectives. I prefer to hold short meetings on a regular basis. That way, I can hold myself to fewer objectives. When I wait to have them on a monthly or quarterly basis, I end up with a runaway train. My staff members tend to look at infrequent meetings like they're the semester test. Shorter, frequent meetings are more like pop quizzes. They can deal with those."

Preventable Problems

Structure begins with something so obvious, its amazing how many meeting leaders fail to do it. It is simply *starting on time.* As a meeting leader, you set the tone for your meeting by being there, or not being there, before anyone enters the room. Your very presence—calmly seated and obviously ready to begin—conveys the clear message that both the meeting and those in attendance are important to you. By rushing in late—after the others are seated—and scrambling to find a starting point, you send a very different message.

Structure also means that you make immediate use of two things you did in your planning: you begin your meeting by clarifying its purpose, and you run it according to your prepared agenda. *You* may know why you've called people together; but if you don't share that information with them, you can't blame them for straying from your objectives. If the meeting's purpose is your destination, its agenda is your road map. It is more than a mere formality. Not only does it help you in your planning, it tests the waters on controversial topics; it informs people of the subject matter to be covered; and it puts time constraints on each topic. Without structure, you can torpedo your meeting in its first five minutes.

Arizona State Representative Becky Jordan attends a lot of meetings, conducts a lot of meetings, and is frustrated by a lot of meetings. Lack of structure and runaway discussions are two of her very pet peeves.

"One of the most important things you need in a meeting is a structured agenda. It should be fairly specific, and it should have time limits for discussion that everybody knows ahead of time. Even Congress does that. Recently, when we were taking the legislature to the people, we were in Prescott, Arizona, to discuss things like rural health care, taxes, economic development, and several other very broad topics. It was like a town meeting. Supposedly, there was an agenda for this meeting; but, if there was, the senator who was conducting it didn't have a clue. People were given speaker slips to fill out specifying what group they were representing and which of the issues they wished to talk about. On the bottom of the speaker slip it said, 'Please limit your comments to five minutes.' No one did. The whole meeting was out of control because most people didn't have a question to ask; they just had a complaint to register. One person went on forever, and the senator just let him talk. I believe that when people come from many miles away, they do deserve their day; and I would have given him that. But then I would have called time and moved on."

But even with structure, how do you avoid *runaway discussions*— the second meeting unraveler? In a runaway discussion, the rules are ignored . . . everyone talks at once . . . heated exchanges break out . . . your objectives fly out the window . . . and you lose control. So, if your carefully planned discussion runs amok, how can you reign it in? Let's take one of a meeting leader's greatest fears: an altercation between two people at the meeting.

Imagine that they are angry at each other. They raise their voices. They lose all sense of decorum. What do you do? Well, as the leader, you have several options. Best-case scenario: when you see the discussion beginning to run away, you can grab the reigns and head it off at the pass. Worst-case scenario: the argument escalates too quickly to prevent damage, and you have to stop what has already begun. First, you could interrupt and take the floor . . .

"Folks, this discussion seems to have taken on a life of its own. Let's see if I can sum up each of your viewpoints. Then we can decide how to proceed from here."

Or, you could call on someone else to speak . . .

"Excuse me, but I'd like to hear from Adrienne on this. She headed up our last project and has a pretty good grasp of our style."

You could ask the combatants to sum up each other's point of view . . .

"So we can clarify this issue, Bob, would you tell us what you think Adrienne is trying to say. If you're wrong, she can correct your misunderstanding. Then, we'll reverse the process and ask her what she thinks you are trying to say."

As a last resort, you could recess the meeting until the adversaries have had a chance to cool down.

"Let's take a 15-minute break and give all of us a chance to sort out our feelings on this subject."

If you don't do any of these things, you will have *abdicated control*—a sure way to let your meeting jump the track. There are two kinds of control—self-control and meeting control. Self-control means you keep your head, stay calm, and don't become part of the problem. Meeting control, on the other hand, focuses on controlling the meeting *process*, not the people at the meeting. Meeting control might involve intervening when the discussion drifts, or veers, off course . . . clarifying fuzzy issues . . . summarizing main points and finding a common thread among them . . . breaking up log jams or arguments . . . or simply cutting off discussion on one topic to move on to another.

Susan Beal at times conducts problem-solving meetings at Eagle Brands—the kind where an issue is put on the table and all of the options and possible solutions are discussed until the best one surfaces. In this type of meeting, particularly, preventable problems are almost predictable.

"When a conflict arises in a meeting, I stop it. If people are spending way too much time arguing, I either break them up and suggest a compromise; or I say, 'Take this outside, and finish it later,' and then move on to the next step. With people who don't talk, I ask them directly, 'What do you think?' For those who won't stop talking, I try to be somewhat polite. I say, 'We've heard from you. Now let's have a chance to hear from a couple of other people on this subject.' "

Lack of structure, runaway discussions, and abdicating control are all potentially serious, but so is derailer number four—*forgetting to close the meeting.* As important as opening the meeting is, closing it correctly is just as important. Don't wait until the last minute to wrap up the discussion and adjourn. If your first act was to announce your purpose, one of your last ones should be to summarize what has been accomplished and, most important, to test those results against your purpose.

Restating results is the first half of your close. It is the half that looks back at the meeting and says, "This is what we did." The other half looks ahead and sets the scene for what is to come by saying, "This is what we are going to do next." Your very last act should be to thank the group for its participation. Even if you don't consider your meeting an unqualified success, try to highlight *something* that went well or produced tangible results. The single most important thing you can do in your close is to acknowledge the contributions of those who attended. This will make them feel personally valued and assure them that their time has been well spent.

These are some of the most common reasons why meetings fail. What is so frustrating is that these things don't have to happen, and you can do a great deal to prevent them. If there is a single area where you do have control, it is that of *planning*. That one is entirely in your hands; and, to a large degree, so are the others. Lack of structure results from lack of planning. Runaway discussions are predictable when your meetings lack structure. Abdicating control is something only you can do. As a meeting leader, you have an obligation to keep your meetings on track. It is your responsibility to control the process, to set the right tone from the beginning, to keep the discussion focused, to move toward your objective, and to respect the contributions and feelings of your group. The more you exercise the right kind of control in your meetings, the less likely you are to forget to close.

Defusing the Land Mines

Those are the *preventable* problems. What about the not-so-preventable ones—the kind that catch even the most seasoned meeting leaders off guard. Think of them as land mines, because you rarely know when you're going to step on one and blow your meeting to bits. If you know what you're looking for, you can learn to spot and defuse them before they explode. Under the heading of land mines we would surely include the three Ds—difficult people, difficult situations, and difficult groups. Let's take just a couple of minutes to describe them, so you'll know them when you see them.

First, *difficult people*: If you took attendance at most meetings, you could identify almost as many archetypes as there are participants. From the King or Queen who insists on running the meeting, to the Dreamer, who keeps drifting off into another world, the cast of characters is fascinating. The ones you probably know best are called the Dominator, who is fighting you for the leadership of *your* meeting . . . Silent Sam or Samantha, the person who melts into the woodwork and doesn't attract any attention . . . and the Socializer, the happy hindrance who is off the subject more than on it, who entertains everyone with irrelevancies, and who agrees with anything and everything anyone says.

What can you do with these difficult people? With the King or Queen and Dominator, you gently but firmly maintain control of your meeting. With the Dreamer and Silent Sam, your challenge is to engage their interest and encourage them to contribute. The Socializer must be kept focused on the subject whenever he or she goes off on a tangent. All of this sounds easier than it is, of course. Handling difficult people in meetings or in life is the subject of another book.

━━━━━━━━━━━━━━━━━━━━━━━━━━━━▶

Becky Jordan chairs a committee and runs a tight meeting. That process is facilitated somewhat by the protocol followed during House committee meetings. For the most part, says Jordan, that protocol heads problems off at the pass; but sometimes the process does break down. When it does, it becomes the meeting leader's responsibility to reestablish order.

"In our meetings in the legislature, there is always a chairman in charge. If I am a chair, and you want to talk to someone, you have to address me first. Once I've recognized you, you will say, 'Madame Chairman' and the other person's name. When that person responds, he also has to go through me. That is the best control in the world because it slows everything down. But when things get a little bit hot and people start going at it across the table, I just bang the gavel and stop it before it starts.

"But I've decided, if I have some of that garbage in my committee next year, I am thinking about just recessing the committee and taking the adversaries outside. Then, I would tell them that I will not tolerate rudeness—not to anyone in my committee, not to lobbyists, not to department employees, and especially not to the public. If they cannot be civil, then I won't recognize them; and they won't speak in my committee. I don't think anyone should have to tolerate rudeness, and I refuse to do so."

━━━━━━━━━━━━━━━━━━━━━━━━━━━━▶

Next, *difficult situations:* Few things make a meeting leader feel more out of control than conflict in the meeting. The only thing worse than observing the conflict is being in the thick of it. Flying off the handle may relieve your tension, but it is more likely to escalate the situation than to diffuse it. If you're not the problem, but others are, you might try using a *process check*—a way of stopping the action in mid-scene to take a look at what is really happening between adversaries.

Finally, *difficult groups:* Sometime meetings drift off course because of group dynamics. Difficult groups range from those characterized by chaos to those suffering from terminal apathy. One kind of difficult group engages in what noted psychologist, author, and academician Irving L. Janis named "groupthink." Groupthink encourages members to believe the group is always right and moral and fosters the illusion that all conclusions reached are unanimous.

In another type of difficult group, as members opt for harmony, everyone has a nice time; but little gets accomplished. Some difficult groups are mired in structure and bureaucracy, and *how* the meeting is conducted takes precedence over *what* gets done. Finally, there is the group that thrives on action and argument. While it does get things done quickly, it often does so without adequate information or exploration of ideas.

The Tip of the Iceberg: The Meeting

Now that we've looked at some of the most frequent and often preventable problems that can sidetrack your efforts, let's talk about the actual meeting. Though we've tried to make the point that premeeting planning is critical to your success, there is no question that what you do *during* the meeting is just as important. Let us assume that you got off to a great start: you were ready and waiting before the others arrived. You greeted everyone by name, announced the purpose of the meeting, distributed copies of your agenda, and opened the discussion. So far, so good. Now you must *manage* your meeting.

Elnor Hickman has managed meetings ranging from a single chapter to an international conference. To her, the key to every aspect of meeting management is good, solid communication. There is no place, no matter how small or how large that meeting, where it does not play a vital role.

"Communication is the heart of meetings because you are working with varying numbers of people, many of whom may be from different cities, different states, even different countries. With our international convention, people attend from all around the world. Communicating effectively is critical; it can make or break a meeting. One of the cardinal rules is *don't take anything for granted.* You may need to touch base two or three times to make sure that what you think everybody knows, they in fact do know. That applies to everything from managing information to managing visual aids. As a meeting leader, it is important that you touch base with all the people you are responsible for so that they, in turn, can touch base with all the people *they're* responsible for. In that way, information flows to all levels and all participants."

There are five key elements to effective meeting management. They are: structuring the discussion, keeping the meeting on track, using visual aids, eliciting information, and creating a team. Let's look at those elements one at a time.

Structured group discussions usually follow a logical sequence, an identifiable pattern. They begin with a question, like: "What happened to the second quarter's numbers?" which is answered by some symptom of the problem: "Sales are down in the Midwest."

Then comes information gathering: "What changed in the Midwest? What is the nature of our competition there? Are our account executives running into problems? Is the Service Department backing up our people in the field?"

Next comes the investigation phase: "What are the latest sales figures? Do they show a trend? Do future orders bear out that trend?"

Then a possible diagnosis: "It could be that our competitors have established a foothold . . . or maybe it's the downturn in the economy."

And, finally, a prescription: "If cutting the budget was the problem, let's have the agency plan a full-scale Midwest campaign next quarter."

Structuring the discussion is the first essential step in achieving your objective. The second is to keep the meeting constantly moving in the direction of that objective. This requires sensitivity, concentration, and discipline—not to mention a number of other guidelines, which may seem a bit larger than life when they are presented in list form. But, we think you'll see that they all make sense and should serve as reminders about things you already know. To keep a meeting on track, first stimulate discussion, and then don't let it lag. Ask questions. Try to balance the discussion by drawing in those who aren't talking and by not letting any single point of view predominate.

Legislator Becky Jordan might add to that list: "Let opposing points of view be aired, and show respect for those who attend the meeting." In legislative committee meetings, the chairman has the authority to recognize—or not to recognize—anyone who wishes to speak. At one unforgettable committee hearing, Representative Jordan recalls, the chair exercised that prerogative but did so at the expense of fair and open discussion.

"The committee was holding hearings on mass transit. At the meeting were a number of people who had come in wheelchairs to testify on behalf of more wheelchair-accessible buses. The chairman would not recognize these people or allow them to speak. They had gone to great lengths to attend; but he, personally, did not want to hear what they had to say. So, he just didn't call on them. As chair, he did have that right; but it was so inconsiderate; to me, it was simply unconscionable."

Use gentle reminders to keep people focused on the topic at hand. As we mentioned earlier, break up controversies before they break up the meeting. Keep things lively but under control.

Focus on key issues and major points. And, of course, never lose sight of your objective. Finally, watch your timetable, finish on time, and make sure there is a real conclusion to the meeting.

This brings us to using visual aids. When you find yourself in a position of presenting information at a meeting, you immediately face two challenges: capturing and holding people's attention and making sure your information is received and understood. You'll have better success with those challenges if you make use of an array of available visual aids to augment and illustrate your work. You may choose to use:

- A blackboard, which brings spontaneity and immediacy to your talk
- An easel or flip-chart, on which you can make notes with markers
- A flannel board with mottoes, pictures, or charts attached
- An opaque projector for sharp, distinct, black-and-white images
- Charts, to help focus attention on key ideas
- Movies, videotapes, slide presentations, filmstrips, or transparencies, for impact and color

Each has advantages and disadvantages; and, of course, they vary in effectiveness, flexibility, and cost. But using the right one can make all the difference between a memorable presentation and one that is simply run of the mill.

━━━━━━━━━━━━━━━━━━━━━━━━━━━━▶

Sue St. John recalls the Monday morning meetings, years ago, where she began as a participant and, ultimately, ended up as the meeting leader. What amazes her, in retrospect, was that these meetings remained constant and consistent from the beginning—before, during, and even beyond her tenure.

"The most productive meetings I've ever experienced were on Monday mornings at a training and consulting firm I worked for. These meetings were only one hour in length, and that was part of their beauty. It was just enough time to see where we were, get focused on where we were going, and get moving. Each person brought her checklist from the week before and reported on what was accomplished and what still needed to be done. Then, the group collectively offered assistance and resources where they were needed; and we mapped out our direction for the next five days. By the time we finished, we each had a plan. It was a totally synergistic thing, where we were all going about our business, yet helping each other. There were no games, no hidden agendas. Sounds corny, but it was like we were the three musketeers, only there were six of us!"

The third element in effective meeting management is your ability to elicit information from those in attendance. If one of the skills you need is presenting information, the other is the ability to obtain it from others. To become a master at information gathering, you need only one tool—*the question.* In fact, the ability to ask the right question at the right time in the right way is the most important skill you can develop as a meeting leader.

Questions will help you do so many of the things you want to do in your meeting, including:

- ▸ Open discussions and get them pointed in the right direction
- ▸ Clarify the nature of a problem
- ▸ Arrive at conclusions
- ▸ Encourage participation
- ▸ Stress important points
- ▸ Gather facts
- ▸ Control your meetings
- ▸ Keep people interested and involved
- ▸ Allow participants to process their feelings and opinions

Quite a job description for what you may once have considered the lowly question. As a meeting leader and as a communicator, your ability to make questions work for you can be one of your greatest assets.

The last essential element in meeting management is to create a team. Meetings bring together diverse groups of people who, in theory, collaborate in pursuit of a common goal. Such a collaborative group is called a *team*, and its collective efforts should produce results greater than any single member, working alone, could ever hope to produce. Teamwork must be a managed, planned, and coordinated effort. When real teamwork occurs, it is not an accident; rather it is the result of time, effort, and self-evaluation. To build a team, you and the members of your group must look at both your *process*—how you are working together—and your *content*—what you are working on. The result of all of this observation and evaluation, ideally, will be a group that pools its efforts to produce results that far exceed the collective input of its members. This is called *synergy*.

Wrapping Up the Meeting

At long last, your meeting is drawing to a close. As we mentioned earlier, simply closing your briefcase and walking out of the room does not qualify as a proper close. The way you close a meeting is every bit as important as the way you close a sales call. In fact, they have much in common. Suppose you went through all the aspects of a well-executed sales call. Everything you did was leading up to the moment when the customer said, "I'll take it. Where do I sign?" If you left before you got to that point, you never really completed the call. Let's look at how all of this equates to closing your meeting.

Before you say the words, "This meeting is adjourned," you have some wrapping up to do. If you began by stating your objective, it seems reasonable to assume you would end by announcing whether or not that objective was achieved. If your group reached a conclusion or solution to a problem, you will want to summarize it verbally and announce that you will follow up with a written summary. If the need for further information was generated, and that information is to come from you, make a commitment to secure, prepare, and send it. If the problem was *not* solved, if all the issues were *not* covered, or if new issues arose during the meeting, propose a follow-up meeting and decide on a date to hold it. The important point here is to bring closure to the meeting.

Besides summing up what has taken place and whether or

not you accomplished what you came together to do, there are a few other things to do. Frequently, meetings end with an agreement or assignment of follow-up tasks. Ask for volunteers, call on someone to do them, or take them on yourself. But, before you take on extra responsibilities, you should be conscious of your own workload, personal schedule, and priorities. If you assign these responsibilities to others, or if others volunteer to handle them, they become accountable, just as you would. Getting people to follow through on meeting-generated tasks is like getting them to show up on time. If you're serious, show it. The close should not leave any doubt in the minds of participants that this activity has been completed.

One reason for following up on assignments is that promises made in meetings are frequently forgotten moments after the meetings end. So, in fact, is nearly everything else—topics covered, conclusions reached, decisions made—which is why it's so important to take minutes. Someone should be responsible for keeping track of what went on, preferably someone who can get the essence of the discussion down on paper accurately and clearly. As the meeting leader, your job is to summarize conclusions and decisions in wording everyone understands and agrees on.

The person taking notes is responsible for recording what you said or wrote on the flip-chart. The minutes will probably be the only accurate record of what took place at the meeting. As such, they should be impersonal, uncritical, and unbiased. Who gets these minutes? They should be distributed to those who attended the meeting, those who were invited but were unable to attend, and others in the organization who have a right and a "need to know" what transpired.

The End or Another Beginning?

The meeting is over, and you are finished. Right? Well, only if this is the last meeting you will ever attend or conduct for the rest of your life. Otherwise, you might want some idea of how it went. After all, you spend a lot of time attending or conducting meetings. In fact, your meeting life may be pretty time-consuming. Whether that is time well spent or time wasted depends on how productive those meetings are. The last thing you do is look at the meetings you attend or conduct and compare them to what you've learned in this session. What if you find just how far off the mark your meetings are? What can you do about it?

Start by knowing that you don't have to live with bad meetings. As a meeting leader or a participant, you have the obligation and the ability to do something about your own meeting life. You begin by simply confronting the issue—getting it out in the open for everyone to see. If your meetings seem to lack direction or just go badly, one of your participants may even bring it up before you do. But, if no one else does, it's up to you. Taking a hard look at the quality of your meetings can feel threatening, not only to others, but to you as well. After all, you plan these meetings; you run them; and, to a degree, you own them. Your ego is very much on the line when you encourage others to candidly express their opinions on how well or poorly you are doing your job.

The best way to begin is by admitting your own discomfort with the quality and productivity of the meetings you conduct. Concede that there is a problem, and ask for help or ideas on how to solve it. If you all agree that a problem does exist, the next step is to spell out exactly what it is. When the problem involves the people who are attempting to solve it, it becomes a much more personal and sensitive issue. Changing the course of your meetings is not something you will accomplish during the first fifteen minutes of a regular meeting, before you move on to your real agenda. You probably won't accomplish it in a single get-together either, but you should plan to devote at least one full meeting to beginning the process.

Summing Up

If you want to get your ideas across; to become a problem solver; to think creatively; to inform, motivate, and teach, you need meeting skills. But meeting skills are not restricted to meetings; we use them everywhere and all the time. The reason meetings were saved for last is because, in meetings—whether you are a participant or the leader—you will make use of almost all of the other skills covered in this book. From listening and speaking to relationship building and interpreting nonverbal cues, a meeting is where they come together, where they are tested and honed in a real laboratory. In fact, if you can conduct a successful meeting, you can probably do just about anything!

As an administrative assistant, and as a professional, you *must* sharpen your communication skills for two reasons: The first is that your present job demands competency in this area. You simply *cannot* execute your responsibilities without these skills. The second is that if you want to grow, either in your position or out of it, you must go beyond mere competence. People who succeed in business have mastered the art of communication in all of its myriad forms.

You have been given a great deal to think about and master in this book—probably more than you can assimilate in one time through it. That is intentional. Communication skills take a lifetime to acquire and hone. Professionally and personally, they are worth the investment. It is the book's goal that you will devote just a tiny portion of that lifetime to using it as an ongoing resource in your career.

Bibliography

Baber, Anne, and Waymon, Lynne. *Great Connections: Small Talk and Networking for Business.* Manassas Park, Va.: Impact Publications, 1992.

Buzzotta, V. R.; Lefton, R. E.; and Sherberg, M. *Improving Productivity Through People Skills.* Cambridge, Mass.: Ballinger Publishing Company, 1980.

Cundiff, Merlyn. *Kinesics: The Power of Silent Command.* West Nyack, N.Y.: Parker Publishing Company, 1972.

David, Flora. *Inside Intuition: What We Know About Nonverbal Communication.* New York: McGraw-Hill, 1973.

Goodman, Danny. *Fear Computers No More.* New York: Brady Publishing, 1993.

Janis, Irving L. *Victims of Groupthink.* Boston: Houghton Mifflin, 1972.

Leeds, Dorothy. *Smart Questions.* New York: McGraw-Hill, 1987.

Nierenberg, Gerard I., and Calero, Henry H. *How to Read a Person Like a Book, and What to Do About It.* New York: Cornerstone Library, 1971.

Steil, L. K.; Barker, L. L.; and Watson, K. W. *Effective Listening: Key to Your Success.* Reading, Mass.: Addison-Wesley, 1983.

Walther, George R. *Phone Power.* New York: Berkley Publishing, 1987.

Zinsser, William. *On Writing Well: An Informal Guide to Nonfiction Writing.* New York: Harper & Row, 1976.

Index